IRON MAN
BOOKS OF KORVAC II
OVERCLOCK

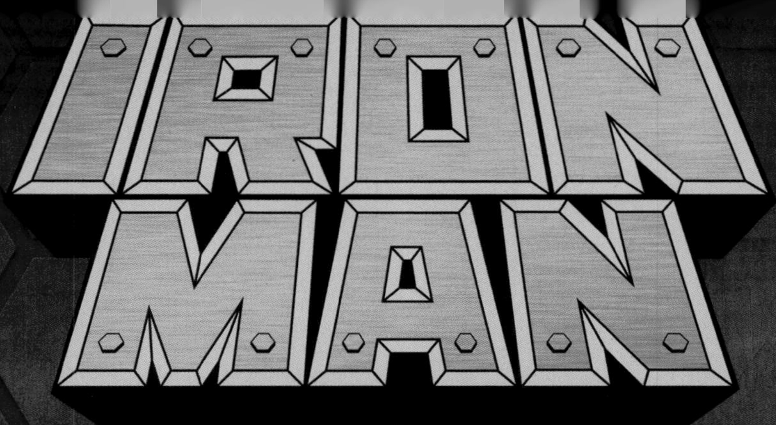

BOOKS OF KORVAC II
OVERCLOCK

CHRISTOPHER CANTWELL
WRITER

CAFU (#6-7, 9-10) &
ANGEL UNZUETA (#8, 11)
ARTISTS

FRANK D'ARMATA
COLOR ARTIST

VC's JOE CARAMAGNA
LETTERER

ALEX ROSS
COVER ART

ALEX ROSS
IRON MAN ARMOR DESIGN

MARTIN BIRO
ASSISTANT EDITOR

ALANNA SMITH
ASSOCIATE EDITOR

TOM BREVOORT
EDITOR

IRON MAN CREATED BY STAN LEE, LARRY LIEBER, DON HECK & JACK KIRBY

COLLECTION EDITOR: **DANIEL KIRCHHOFFER**
ASSISTANT MANAGING EDITOR: **MAIA LOY**
ASSISTANT MANAGING EDITOR: **LISA MONTALBANO**
SENIOR EDITOR, SPECIAL PROJECTS: **JENNIFER GRÜNWALD**

VP, PRODUCTION & SPECIAL PROJECTS: **JEFF YOUNGQUIST**
BOOK DESIGNER: **STACIE ZUCKER**
SVP PRINT, SALES & MARKETING: **DAVID GABRIEL**
EDITOR IN CHIEF: **C.B. CEBULSKI**

RON MAN VOL. 2: BOOKS OF KORVAC II — OVERCLOCK. Contains material originally published in magazine form as IRON MAN (2020) #6-11. First printing 2021. ISBN 978-1-302-92552-9. Published by MARVEL WORLDWIDE, INC., a ubsidiary of MARVEL ENTERTAINMENT, LLC. OFFICE OF PUBLICATION: 1290 Avenue of the Americas, New York, NY 10104. © 2021 MARVEL No similarity between any of the names, characters, persons, and/or institutions in this magazine vith those of any living or dead person or institution is intended, and any such similarity which may exist is purely coincidental. **Printed in Canada.** KEVIN FEIGE, Chief Creative Officer; DAN BUCKLEY, President, Marvel Entertainment; JOE QUESADA, EVP & Creative Director; DAVID BOGART, Associate Publisher & SVP of Talent Affairs; TOM BREVOORT, VP, Executive Editor; NICK LOWE, Executive Editor, VP of Content, Digital Publishing; DAVID GABRIEL, VP of Print & Digital Publishing; JEFF YOUNGQUIST, VP of Production & Special Projects; ALEX MORALES, Director of Publishing Operations; DAN EDINGTON, Managing Editor; RICKEY PURDIN, Director of Talent Relations; JENNIFER GRÜNWALD, Senior Editor, Special Projects; SUSAN CRESPI, Production Manager; STAN LEE, Chairman Emeritus. For information regarding advertising in Marvel Comics or on Marvel.com, please contact Vit DeBellis, Custom Solutions & Integrated Advertising Manager, at vdebellis@ ...el.com. For Marvel subscription inquiries, please call 888-511-5480. **Manufactured between 8/6/2021 and 9/7/2021 by SOLISCO PRINTERS, SCOTT, QC, CANADA.**

THIS ISN'T ME.
THIS ISN'T ME.
THIS HURTS.
THIS HURTS.
SOMETHING'S BROKEN.
SOMETHING'S BROKEN.
I HAVE TO FIX IT. I WILL.
I DON'T KNOW IF I CAN FIX IT. NOT THIS TIME.

I'M DONE BEING POLITE.
ALL IT'S GOTTEN ME IS A BROKEN NECK.
WAIT...
MY MIND IS BROKEN AGAIN.

WAIT...
PATSY.

TONY.

WAM

WAM

HRRRRRRRRRRR!
NYC TAXI
GA-DNKK
AAAAAA!

DRIVE! NOW!

NO HOSPITAL...
YOU HAVE TO--
...NECK'S BROKEN, ARMOR HOLDING IT TOGETHER... NEED--A... A TECHNICIAN... LIKE...

"...HALCYON."
...THE HELL HAPPENED?
SOMETHING WENT BOOM... SOMETHING REALLY BIG.

AREN'T YOU SUPPOSED TO HAVE THAT SPIDER-SENSE JUNK, SCARLET?
WELL, MISTY, FORGIVE ME IF I ASSUMED IT WAS GOING OFF BECAUSE WE WERE ABOUT TO RUN INTO SOME HENCHMEN OR, DARE I SAY, A NASTY OL' KORVAC.

THE FORTUNATE NEWS IS...YOU'RE NOT DEAD.
GARGOYLE, HOLY #$%&.

THE HECK HAPPENED? WHAT DID HE DO?
DAMN, HE'S LOST A WHOLE WING. HE'S HURT BAD.
HE SHIELDED US WITH BIO-MYSTICAL ENERGY. HE DRAWS IT FROM HIS OWN LIFE FORCE.
WHUMP

THEN BY THAT SIMPLE MATH--EXPLOSION PLUS DRAINED LIFE ENERGY--WE'VE GOTTA GET HIM HELP BEFORE HE DIES.

VWOOOOM
BLIZZARD, T-MINUS WHAT?
4 MINUTES AND 23 SECONDS UNTIL LAUNCH.
WEAPONS INVENTORY CHECK COMPLETE.
WE'LL NEED IT ALL ONCE WE REACH TAA II.
THE DEFENSES GALACTUS HAS BUILT ON HIS WORLDSHIP ARE NOTHING SHORT OF DEVASTATING.

I'M GOING TO SAY GOODBYE TO COLONEL RHODES. THEN WE CLOSE UP SHOP ON EARTH.
OUR FINAL CRUSADE...
LORD KORVAC.
GUARDSMAN. I'M GLAD YOU'RE FINALLY WITH US, BROTHER.
I'M HONORED TO BE WITH YOU.
GOOD. STRAP IN. DESTINY AWAITS.
C'MON, OL' NEW YORK PLUMBING... C'MON, OL' RHODEY... FIGHT IT... GIMME SOMETHIN' HERE...
CRAK!
COLONEL, I WON'T ALLOW THAT!

ZZZZZBBEEOOOWWWFFM
THIS WON'T DO. HE'LL ALERT OTHERS. I'LL HAVE MY HANDS FULL ON TAA II--I CAN'T RISK AN ATTACK BY SOME CONTINGENT OF EARTHLY IGNORANCE.

LET ME GO. I'LL TAKE CARE OF HIM.
GUARDSMAN, I NEED YOU WITH US--YOU'VE SERVED ME WELL--
THIS IS HOW I SERVE.

YOUR FAITH IS UNWAVERING.
REMEMBER ME AT ASCENSION.
MOST ASSUREDLY. YOU'LL FEEL IT IN YOUR VERY SOUL.

DO NOT FAIL IN THIS, BROTHER!

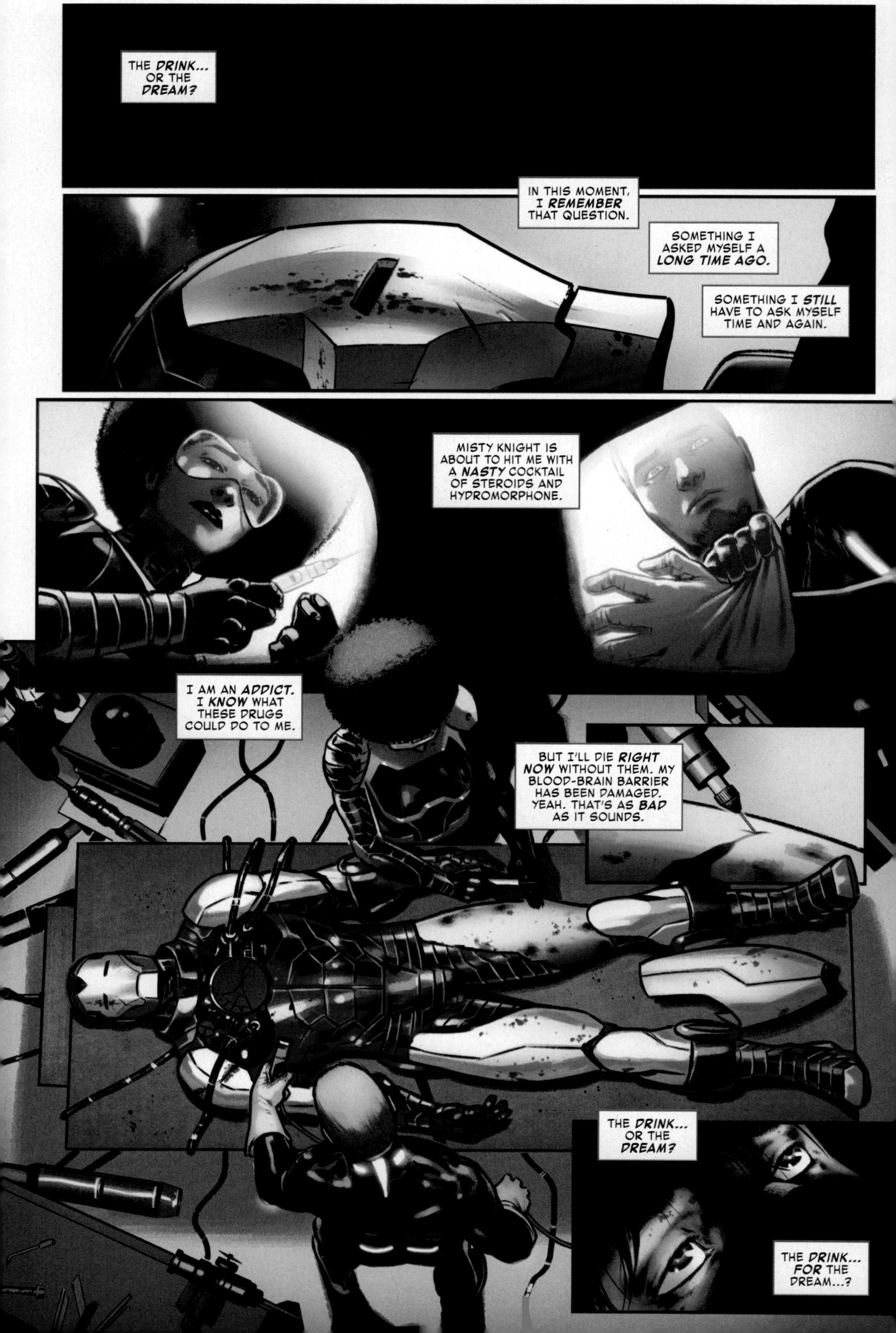

THE *DRINK*... OR THE *DREAM?*

IN THIS MOMENT, I *REMEMBER* THAT QUESTION.

SOMETHING I ASKED MYSELF A *LONG TIME AGO.*

SOMETHING I *STILL* HAVE TO ASK MYSELF TIME AND AGAIN.

MISTY KNIGHT IS ABOUT TO HIT ME WITH A *NASTY* COCKTAIL OF STEROIDS AND HYDROMORPHONE.

I AM AN *ADDICT.* I *KNOW* WHAT THESE DRUGS COULD DO TO ME.

BUT I'LL DIE *RIGHT NOW* WITHOUT THEM. MY BLOOD-BRAIN BARRIER HAS BEEN DAMAGED. YEAH. THAT'S AS *BAD* AS IT SOUNDS.

THE *DRINK*... OR THE *DREAM?*

THE *DRINK*... *FOR* THE DREAM...?

NOW HALCYON IS FUSING MY ARMOR'S CERVICAL COLUMN RINGS TOGETHER. THIS WILL STABILIZE THE SPINAL INJURY AND PREVENT ME FROM SUFFOCATING. KID'S NOT BAD AT THIS.
NOW HE'S TORQUING THE INTERIOR CHASSIS STRUCTURE OF MY NECK TO 113 FOOT-POUNDS.
CRRRRRIICKT
CRRRRICCKT
THIS WILL FURTHER STABILIZE THE FRACTURE. MY HEAD'S RANGE OF MOTION WILL BE LIMITED TO 50 DEGREES OF ROTATION.
WITHOUT THE MEDS, THE PAIN FROM THE CUMULATIVE TRAUMA WOULD IMMEDIATELY SEND ME INTO SHOCK.
I CAN'T TAKE MY ARMOR OFF UNTIL I'M READY TO BE PREPPED FOR EMERGENCY SURGERY. THAT'S NOT HAPPENING ANYTIME SOON.
EVEN REMOVING MY HELMET RIGHT NOW WOULD PROVE FATAL.

I AM ALIVE.
I AM ANGRY.
I AM NO LONGER APOLOGIZING FOR ANYTHING.
NOT MY MACHINES. NOT MY DECISIONS. NOT MY DEEDS.
I AM GOING TO WIN THIS FIGHT. I AM THE ONE WHO WINS.
KORVAC THINKS HE IS GOD.
BUT I AM IRON MAN.

FROG-MAN, HOW'S GARGOYLE?
HE'S STILL **REGENERATING.** HE LOST A LOT OF...**BIOLOGICAL MATERIAL.**
WHAT'S HIS E.T.A.?
HIS **E.T.A.?**

*ON **RECOVERY.** I NEED HIM UP AND AMBULATORY.*

WHAT DO YOU WANT ME TO SAY? HE'S A #$%& ***GARGOYLE.*** YOU WANT ME TO ***GOOGLE*** IT?

*WE'RE LEAVING THE PLANET INSIDE OF **TWO HOURS.** IF HE'S OUT FOR THE COUNT, THEN HE'S A **WASTE** OF MY TIME, AND WE **LEAVE HIM.***

OOOOKAY, MR. SHELL-HEAD...
I CAN ACTUALLY THINK OF A WAY MORE APPROPRIATE MODIFIER FOR ***"HEAD"*** RIGHT NOW.

I DON'T WANT TO GO BACK.
PLEASE DON'T MAKE ME GO BACK.
YOU DON'T HAVE TO.
I FORGIVE YOU, PATSY. I ALWAYS WILL. JUST FOLLOW ME.
TO WHERE, KORVAC? YOU SAY YOU'RE A SAVIOR.
WHAT DOES YOUR PARADISE EVEN LOOK LIKE?

IT LOOKS LIKE THIS.
PEACE. HARMONY. EVERYWHERE.
THE BREEZE IS... SWEET...AND WARM...
WHAT DID YOU THINK MY UNIVERSE WOULD LOOK LIKE?
PATSY. HOW DO YOU FEEL?
I FEEL LIKE I JUST HAD TWO INJECTIONS OF OLANZAPINE. HOW ABOUT YOU?

I'M SWIMMING IN PAIN MEDS. FEELS GREAT, BUT THAT MIGHT BE A PROBLEM LATER.
WELL, RIGHT NOW...I GENERALLY KNOW WHERE I AM. BUT...KORVAC'S STILL IN HERE. AND HE'S REALLY...TOSSING THE PLACE.
TONY... WHAT IF HE'S RIGHT?
HE'S NOT.
IT COULD BE BEAUTIFUL.
IT WOULDN'T BE.
KORVAC CAN'T CREATE A PERFECT UNIVERSE.
HELL, I BET YOU I COULD CREATE A BETTER UNIVERSE THAN KORVAC.
NOW YOU'RE SCARING ME.

THIS IS LOOKING MORE AND MORE LIKE A SUICIDE MISSION. IRON MAN COULD GET US ALL KILLED.
BUT IF HE AND HELLCAT GO ALONE, THEY'LL GET THEMSELVES KILLED, WITH THE SHAPE THEY'RE IN.
AND KORVAC DOES WHAT HE WANTS, THEN SAY GOODBYE TO LIFE AS YOU KNOW IT. IF WE ALL GO, THERE'S A BETTER CHANCE OF STOPPING HIM.
WHAT ABOUT CAPTAIN AMERICA OR SOMEBODY? AREN'T THERE LIKE 467 DIFFERENT AVENGERS AND LIKE EIGHT SEPARATE TEAMS?
BY THE TIME THEY GET THEIR ACT TOGETHER, WE'LL BE LIGHT-YEARS AWAY.
HALCYON SAYS... "DON'T YOU GUYS SOMETIMES WORK WITH PEOPLE FROM OUTER SPACE?"
THAT'S...A DAMN GOOD POINT. SOMEONE OFF-WORLD COULD INTERCEPT US.
I CAN TRY TO GET A COVERT SIGNAL OUT ONCE WE LEAVE EARTH.
NOBODY HERE IS LEAVING EARTH.
THERE'S A NEW SENIOR OFFICER ASSIGNED. ME.
I'M GETTING THE WHOLE CAVALRY TO RIDE AGAINST THIS DUDE. YOU ALL NEED TO CALL IT A DAY.
RHODEY. DAMN GLAD TO SEE YOU. BUT THIS IS MY FIGHT. MINE.

THE HELL IT IS. LOOK AT YOU. YOU'RE THE LAST PERSON WHO SHOULD BE TAKING ON KORVAC RIGHT NOW.
DID HE TELL YOU HIS NECK IS BROKEN? 'CAUSE THAT'S COOL.
I ALREADY CALLED IN BACKUP, TONY. YOU NEED TO TAG OUT--
ENERGY WEAPONS ARE USELESS AGAINST KORVAC, SO I'M GONNA TRY GOOD OLD-FASHIONED BRUTE FORCE--
TONY, GO HOME!
DO NOT GET IN MY WAY, JAMES--
KCHAAKFFFSSSH

THIS IS YOUR LAST NIGHT ON EARTH, RHODES!
HEY, YOU'RE... ALL STILL ALIVE. ALL OF YOU.
HUH. HOW 'BOUT THAT.
TONY...HEY, MAYBE GIVE THE GUY A BREAK, MAN...
YOU WANNA TUSSLE, BIG GUY? LET'S TUSSLE--
KAPOW

KAERSCH
KAERSCH
KAERSCH
WHAT? I GAVE HIM A BREAK.
RHODEY. YOU'RE GOING TO BE MY PILOT ON THIS.
I TOLD YOU OTHERS ARE GONNA HANDLE IT!
YOU KNOW YOU'RE NOT GONNA STOP ME. SO YOU'RE EITHER WITH ME... OR NOT.
...FINE. MAYBE I CAN AT LEAST KEEP YOU FROM GETTING YOURSELF KILLED.
GOOD. NOW BRING ME THE MOST BLEEDING-EDGE, SOPHISTICATED AND TECHNOLOGICALLY ADVANCED SPACECRAFT I OWN.
WE'RE GOING TO MAKE UP FOR LOST TIME.

YOU THINK HALCYON CAN HANDLE THE CONTROLS ON HIS OWN FOR A SECOND?
"YOU KIDDING ME? HE'S FLYING HIS FIRST FASTER-THAN-LIGHT DRIVE ENGINE. KID'S HAVING THE TIME OF HIS LIFE."

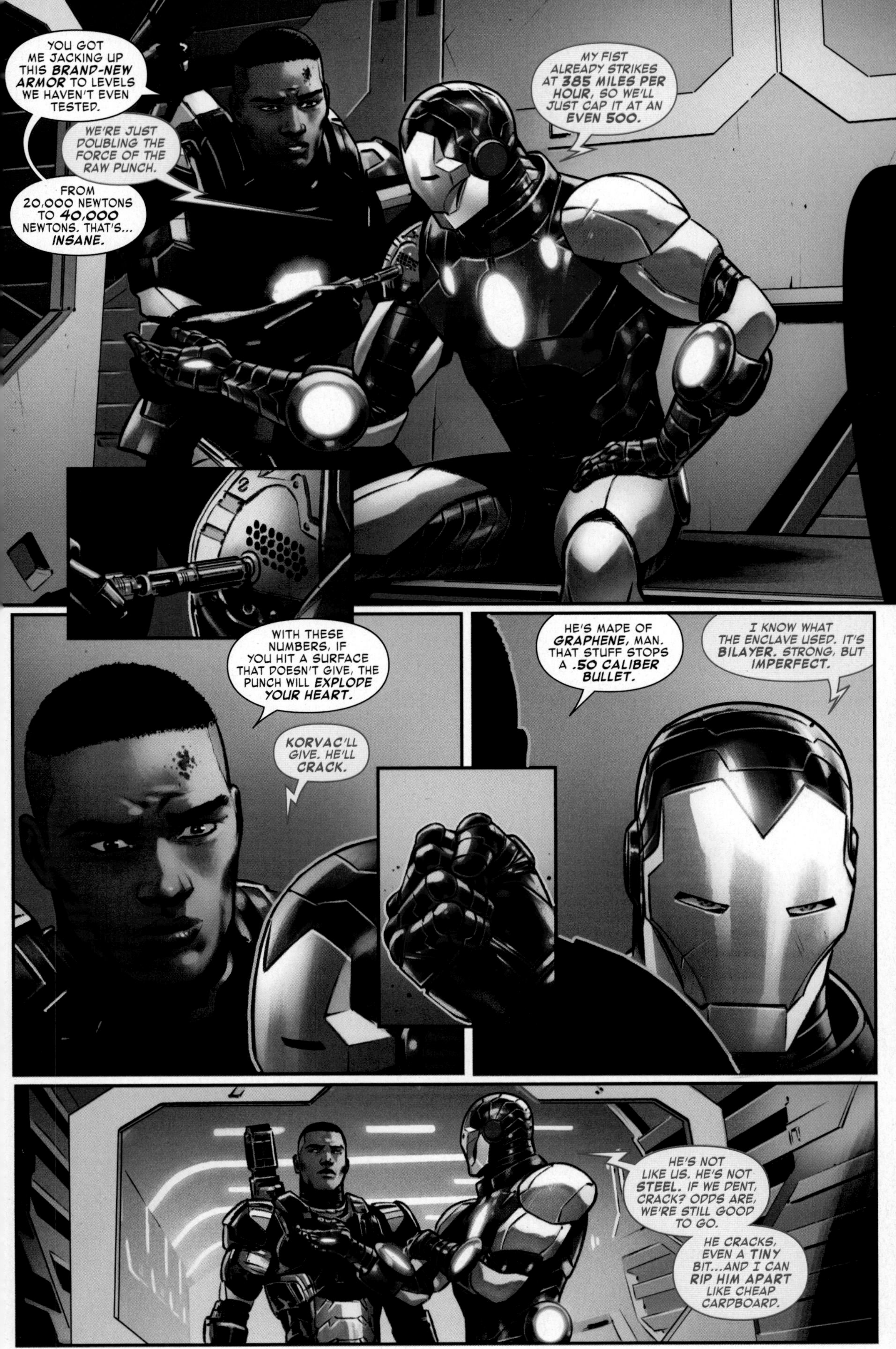
YOU GOT ME JACKING UP THIS BRAND-NEW ARMOR TO LEVELS WE HAVEN'T EVEN TESTED.
MY FIST ALREADY STRIKES AT 385 MILES PER HOUR, SO WE'LL JUST CAP IT AT AN EVEN 500.
WE'RE JUST DOUBLING THE FORCE OF THE RAW PUNCH.
FROM 20,000 NEWTONS TO 40,000 NEWTONS. THAT'S... INSANE.
WITH THESE NUMBERS, IF YOU HIT A SURFACE THAT DOESN'T GIVE, THE PUNCH WILL EXPLODE YOUR HEART.
KORVAC'LL GIVE. HE'LL CRACK.
HE'S MADE OF GRAPHENE, MAN. THAT STUFF STOPS A .50 CALIBER BULLET.
I KNOW WHAT THE ENCLAVE USED. IT'S BILAYER. STRONG, BUT IMPERFECT.
HE'S NOT LIKE US. HE'S NOT STEEL. IF WE DENT, CRACK? ODDS ARE, WE'RE STILL GOOD TO GO.
HE CRACKS, EVEN A TINY BIT...AND I CAN RIP HIM APART LIKE CHEAP CARDBOARD.

YOU'RE GONNA GET YOURSELF *KILLED.* KORVAC IS PURE *ENERGY.*

RIGHT. ENERGY WEAPONS WON'T WORK. BUT I CAN *HIT HIM HARD.*

PLUS I HAVE *BACKUP.*

THANKS, MISTY. CROSSING FINGERS OVER HERE.
WE NEED A TEAM NAME. LIKE...*STAR WARRIORS?*
WAY TOO CLOSE TO *STAR WARS.* BESIDES, WE'RE NOT A TEAM, FROG-MAN. WE'RE MORE LIKE...*EMPLOYEES* OF TONY STARK.

ARE YOU TAKING ABOUT A GOD OR THE GOD?

IS THERE A DIFFERENCE AT THIS POINT?

IT'S ALL CELLS, MOLECULES AND ATOMS. "YOU" ARE THE SUM TOTAL OF MUSCULAR REFLEXES HOLDING YOUR BODY TOGETHER THAT ENDS UP THINKING IT'S SOMETHING...WHICH IS TO SAY SOMEONE.

SO...THE IDEA OF ME...IT'S LIKE... A SIDE EFFECT OF BEING ALIVE?

EXACTLY. HARD SCIENCE. THAT'S IT.

HEAR THAT? THE TEST TUBE CLONE SAYS IT'S JUST SCIENCE.

...
LOOK, MAN.

GOD IS BALANCE. BALANCE... IS SOMETHING SACRED. DELICATE. BUT POWERFUL. THE SCALES ARE ALWAYS TIPPING, AND THEY HAVE TO BE REBALANCED. CONSTANTLY.
THAT IS WHAT WE DO. WE WORK...WE FIGHT... TO REBALANCE. IT IS OUR VOCATION.
WE TAKE OUR CELLS, MOLECULES, ATOMS... AND WE DEDICATE OURSELVES TO BALANCE.
THAT IS HOW WE WORSHIP THIS UNIVERSE AND TREAT IT WITH REVERENCE.
WOW. GARGOYLE WITH THE MIC DROP.
"KORVAC SHOWED ME WHAT HE WANTS TO DO TO ALL OF EXISTENCE."

HE SHOWED IT TO YOU?
WELL, NOT SO MUCH SHOWED. MORE LIKE... PREVIEWED.
HE'S REALLY IN YOUR HEAD, ISN'T HE?
YES. AND THAT MEANS HE KNOWS WE'RE COMING. HE KNOWS WHERE WE ARE.
I WASN'T PLANNING ON AMBUSHING HIM.
THAT MEANS HE'LL BE READY.
SO WILL I.
IT'D BE NICE TO KISS YOU RIGHT NOW.
IT WOULD BE. BUT I CAN'T TAKE THIS STUPID BUCKET OFF MY HEAD. SMALL MATTER OF A BROKEN NECK...

THAT WAS A *WHILE AGO*...AND I *KINDA* GOT MY DRIVER'S LICENSE REVOKED...

I KNOW YOU. YOU CAN HANDLE IT. C'MON, IT'S WORTH A SHOT.

REMOTE QUADRANT ZULU. GOSS SECTOR BORDER.
THEY ARE GAINING, KORVAC.
NOT ONLY DOES STARK HAVE AN FTL, BUT IT'S MORE POWERFUL THAN OURS.
HE HAD YEARS TO DEVELOP HIS BLIZZARD. I BUILT MINE IN FOUR WEEKS.
I...DON'T MEAN TO CRITICIZE--
OF COURSE NOT, DONALD. WE JUST CAN'T AFFORD TO WANE IN OUR FAITH, ELSE WE LOSE SIGHT OF THE TRUTH, YES?
MMMMMPH!
BROTHER MILOS, DECELERATE AND DRAW THEM CLOSER INTO THIS SECTOR.
THEN WE'LL DESTROY THEM. I NEED ZERO THOUGHT OF THEM IN MY MIND AS WE BOARD TAA II.
...YOU...?

LOOKS LIKE THIS ROAD ISN'T JUST ONE WAY, HUH?
HOW DID YOU...?
I USED TO HAVE PRETTY KEEN PSIONIC ABILITIES. GUESS WITH ALL YOUR FIDDLING YOU STIRRED UP THE OL' MIND POT.
EVEN IF I WOULD DEIGN TO LET YOU ACCESS MY THOUGHTS, DO YOU THINK YOU COULD EVEN BEGIN TO UNDERSTAND THEM?
HEY, PAL, I WAS ALMOST VALEDICTORIAN IN HIGH SCHOOL, SO MIND YOUR Ps AND Qs.*
PLUS SHE HAS MY HELP.
*SEE PATSY AND HEDY #95. --TOM
TONY...NICE TO SEE YOU. HOW'S THE NECK?
FINE, THANKS FOR ASKING. IMPRESSIVE FTL DRIVE BY THE WAY, ALTHOUGH IT SEEMS MINE IS A LITTLE FASTER.
OKAY, LET'S NOT START MEASURING EACH OTHER'S FTL DRIVES...
NEITHER OF YOU CAN HURT ME LIKE THIS. YOUR MINDS ARE SCATTERED. EXHAUSTED. TOO ANGRY.
AND YOUR SHIP IS GOING TO BE BLOWN APART IN MINUTES.
THEN WE STILL HAVE A LITTLE TIME FOR YOU TO SHOW ME THIS UTOPIA YOU PLAN TO CREATE.

PATSY'S ALREADY GOTTEN A GLIMPSE.
RIGHT, BUT I'M SURE IT'S NOT ALL JUST ONE BIG THOMAS KINKADE PAINTING.
I WANT TO KNOW HOW IT ACTUALLY WORKS. THE NUTS AND BOLTS OF UNIVERSAL HARMONY.

YOU... REALLY WANT TO KNOW?

I ASKED, DIDN'T I?

YOU'RE... SINCERE. I NEVER EXPECTED...
WHAT?

I NEVER CONSIDERED THAT YOU'D WANT ME TO...SHARE MY VISION WITH YOU...
IT'S QUITE... IT'S QUITE BEAUTIFUL, YOU KNOW...
IT'S PERFECT.

IT'S SIMPLE. ALL THINGS WILL BECOME THE AGGREGATE. ONE SINGLE ENTITY.

WHAT ENTITY?
YOU?

NO. IN THIS UTOPIA THERE IS NO ME.
I BECOME A SEAMLESS PART OF THE AGGREGATE, AS DOES EVERYTHING.
I DON'T BUY THAT FOR A SECOND.

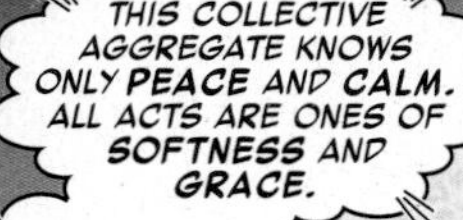
THIS COLLECTIVE AGGREGATE KNOWS ONLY PEACE AND CALM. ALL ACTS ARE ONES OF SOFTNESS AND GRACE.

UNIVERSAL GOOD IS OMNIPRESENT AND OWNED BY NO INDIVIDUAL, NOT EVEN MYSELF.
THE SELF MELTS AWAY COMPLETELY. IT SERVES ONLY THE AGGREGATE.
MEANING YOU.
NO. SOMETHING GREATER. ALL WILL MELD.

SHOW ME THIS AGGREGATE.

ALL ENTROPY WILL BE REVERSED.
SAMENESS. ONENESS. UNITY.
NO HATE. FEAR. WAR.
NONE OF THE ANCIENT EVILS.

WHAT ARE THOSE THINGS?
LIVING EXTENSIONS OF THE AGGREGATE. FLAWLESS IN EVERY CONCEIT.
IS THIS ONE EXAMPLE OF NEW LIFE-FORMS?
NO, THIS IS ALL LIFE ITSELF IN ITS NEW CONCEPTION. ACROSS THE UNIVERSE.
SO...IT'S ENTIRELY HOMOGENOUS. LIMITED ONLY TO THIS SINGULAR TYPE OF EXISTENCE. NO FREEDOM, NO FLARE, NO DEVIATION...NOT EVEN... COLOR.
JUST... NOTHING THINGS GRAZING ON... NOTHING.

I'M SORRY, BUT THIS UTOPIA SUCKS.
THIS IS IT? THIS IS WORTH DEATH AND MURDER? SO WE ALL GET TO BE... CRYSTALS EATING CRYSTALS?
HOW DARE YOU CRITIQUE ME? YOURS IS AN OPINION OF A...A...PROKARYOTE! A MICROBE! BACTERIUM!
YOU SUFFER BECAUSE YOU GRASP ONLY FOR SURVIVAL. YOU CAN'T SEE BEYOND THAT, WHICH IS WHY I HAVE TO DO IT FOR YOU.
YOU'RE WELCOME. YOU'RE LUCKY YOU HAVE ME TO CARE FOR YOU.
BIG K, I DON'T MEAN TO #$%& IN YOUR WIZARD HAT, BUT THE AGGREGATE, THE GLASS CREATURES? THIS IS ALL ABOUT YOU. IT'S OBVIOUSLY--CRINGINGLY--ABOUT YOU.
IT'S A VANITY PROJECT, AND IF YOU WORKED FOR ME...I'D FIRE YOUR ASS.

VEAAAA
OOM
TONY? TONY?!
OH, I SEE...YOU COWARD...
WHAT DID YOU DO TO HIM?!
ME?! NOTHING. NOTHING AT ALL!
YOU DOUBT ME AS A SAVIOR? YOU THINK ALL THIS IS JUST SOME SILLY WHIM?
ZVRREOOOMMMM
THEN EXPERIENCE IT FOR YOURSELF.

TONY! WHAT THE HELL JUST--
I CAME IN HERE AND TONY WAS THERE, AND THEN HE... HELLCAT!
BLIZZARD, GET TO THE AFT CANNONS AND HAVE THE CONTROLLER PREPARE ALL MISSILE CHAMBERS. NOW.
UNICORN, COME AROUND SHARPLY... I'M GOING TO STOMP THESE BUGS OUT OF EXISTENCE.

OKAY, WE FINALLY GOT A VISUAL...

AND HERE THEY COME...FAST... DAMN...

RHODEY! TONY'S GONE!

GONE?!
RIGHT AS I FOUND HIM, HE JUST...BLINKED OUT OF EXISTENCE. AND HELLCAT'S ALL FRIED UP AGAIN--
HOLD UP. WE'RE ABOUT TO HAVE A DAMN DOGFIGHT IN OUTER $#%# SPACE...
"...I NEED GUNNERS IN THE BELLY AND TAIL!"
TSWAOZCH
TSWAOZCH
TSWAOZCH
TSWAOZCH
DAMMIT! EVASIVE MANEUVERS, KID! FLOOR IT AND TIE THESE BASTARDS UP IN A KNOT!
DAMMIT! EVASIVE M
FLOOR IT AND TIE TH
UP IN A KNOT!

ZWAP
...WHAT THE HELL...?
<LOCATION. UNMAPPED.> <NO KNOWN REF FILES.> <SEARCHING... NO RESULTS.><FOLLOWING SYSTEMS HINDERED: FLIGHT. WI-FI ACCESS.>
WHERE IS THIS...? MY JET BOOTS DON'T EVEN WORK...
ONE MOMENT I'M IN KORVAC'S MIND...ON MY SHIP...THEN...
DID HE DO THIS? DID HE SEND ME HERE?

I DON'T EVEN KNOW WHAT SYSTEM THIS IS, LET ALONE PLANET. OR GALAXY. IS THIS...EVEN... REALITY?
HEY, MAYBE I'M DEAD. AGAIN. GREAT.
IT SURE WOULD HELP CLEAR THINGS UP IF THERE WERE AT LEAST ONE OTHER SINGLE LIVING THING OUT HERE--
DON'T MOVE! COLONY PATROL!
TRESPASSER. LOCATORS REPORT YOU TRIPPED THE PERIMETER A WAYS BACK. YOU'RE A NON-AUTHORIZED, WHICH MEANS WE'RE TAKIN' YA IN, LESSIN' YA WANT US TO NEUTRONIZE YA RIGHT HERE, EH?
ARE YOU... CANADIAN...?

I CAN'T SHAKE THEM OFF, BUT IF I CAN GET US IN MISSILE RANGE, WE MIGHT JUST HAVE A SHOT... LITERALLY!
HALCYON, LOAD UP EVERYTHING WE HAVE... SCARLET SPIDER, MISTY--I REALLY NEED YOU TO LAY DOWN MORE COVER FIRE BACK THERE...
TREOWM TREOWM
WHAT DO YOU THINK I'M DOING, RHODES--BALANCING MY CHECKBOOK?
IF KORVAC'S SHIP DOESN'T BACK OFF, WE'LL HAVE NO ROOM FOR A MISSILE SHOT--
IF KORVAC'S SHIP DOESN'T BACK OFF, ITS TAIL FIN IS GONNA BE FLOSSING MY TEETH...
TREOWM
TREOWM TREOWM
DO THEY HAVE MISSILES?
MOST LIKELY.
WELL, SINCE THEY'RE ON OUR ASS LIKE A TIGHT PAIR OF SLACKS, WHATEVER THEY FIRE AT US IS GONNA HIT ME FIRST, SO I'D APPRECIATE SOME EVASIVE MANEUVERS THAT ARE A LITTLE MORE EVASIVE.

GAEGH! I JUST LOST FLIGHT CONTROL... THIS SHIP MANEUVERS LIKE MY GRANDMA'S DAMN CADILLAC!

HALCYON, BREAK US HARD LEFT!

DO IT, KID--NOW OR NEVER...
ISSILE LOAD PRIMED
READY
64 % TARGET LOCK
I'VE GOT YOU, PATSY. HOLD ON...

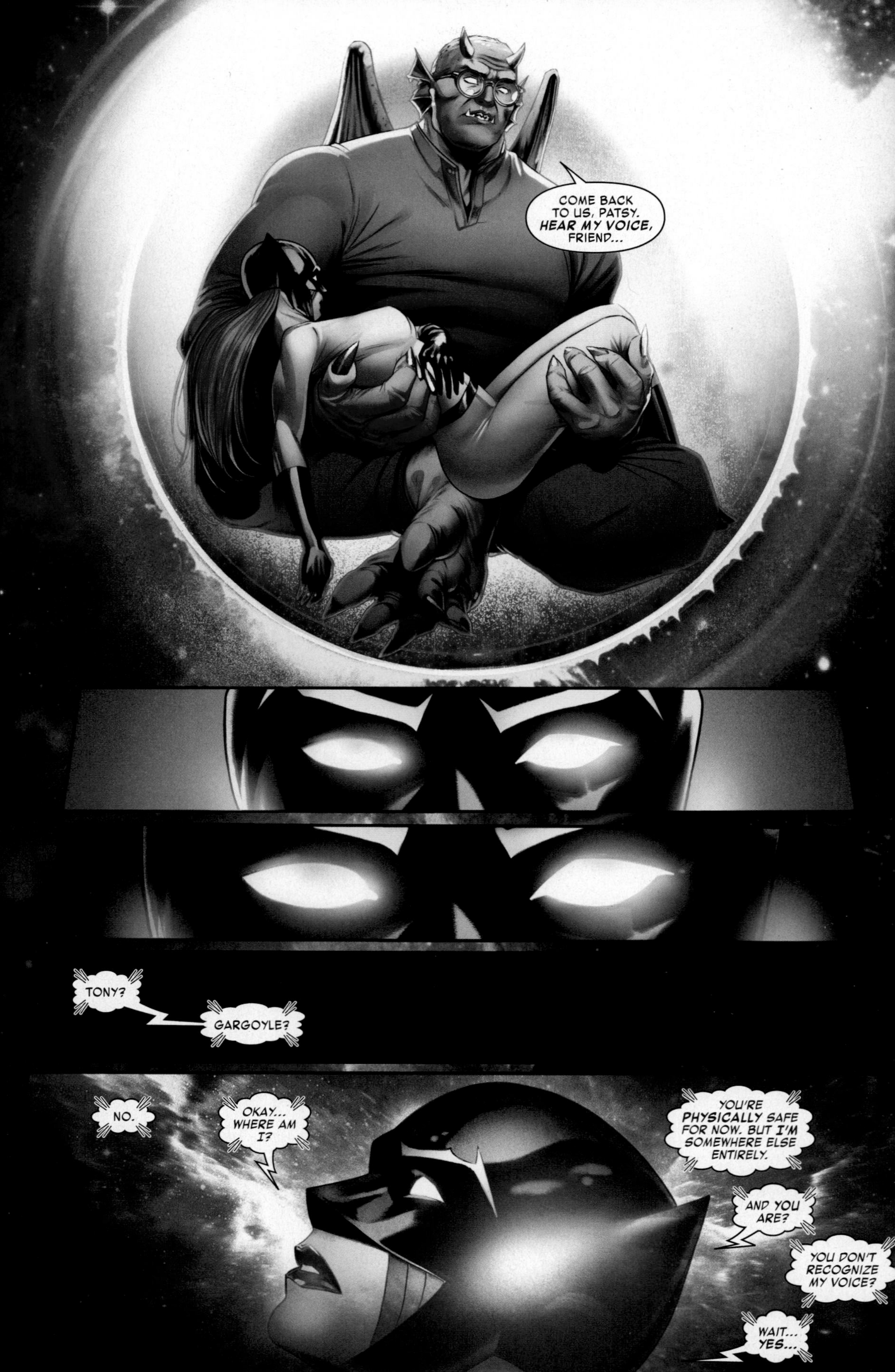
COME BACK TO US, PATSY. HEAR MY VOICE, FRIEND...
TONY?
GARGOYLE?
NO.
OKAY... WHERE AM I?
YOU'RE PHYSICALLY SAFE FOR NOW. BUT I'M SOMEWHERE ELSE ENTIRELY.
AND YOU ARE?
YOU DON'T RECOGNIZE MY VOICE?
WAIT... YES...

MOONDRAGON.
YOU TOOK MY POWERS AWAY A WHILE AGO.* SO I'M SURE YOU'RE NOT TOO THRILLED THAT I'M ACCESSING THE OL' PSYCHOACTIVE RADIO WAVES AGAIN...
HELLO, HELLCAT. IT'S BEEN A WHILE. AND IT SEEMS YOUR MIND HAS REKINDLED SOME...INTERESTING ABILITIES AGAIN.
NO, PATSY.
I'M HERE TO MAKE YOU STRONGER.
*IN DEFENDERS #77. --TOM

I'VE FELT THE THREAT OF KORVAC. THE GUARDIANS AND I ARE FAR FROM YOU, BUT EVEN HERE I SENSE HIM. I'VE SEEN HIS MURDEROUSNESS. HE MUST BE STOPPED.

I'M GOING TO ENHANCE YOUR MENTAL POWERS...BUT I DON'T WANT YOU TO BE HURT, LIKE LAST TIME.

HONESTLY, I... I DON'T KNOW IF THAT'S A GOOD IDEA.

KORVAC WANTS TO ENSLAVE US ALL. NO ONE THING GETS TO DECIDE WHAT ALL THAT IS BECOMES.
I...I DON'T WANT TO LOSE MY MIND AGAIN. I'VE ALREADY COME TOO CLOSE.
I'M HERE TO MAKE YOU STRONGER. SO LET'S START SOMEWHERE MORE FAMILIAR.
ENTERVILLE HIGH SCHOOL
OH MY GOSH! MY OLD HIGH SCHOOL!
YES. AND THE UNIVERSE ALSO TELLS ME YOU ONCE HAD A VERY GOOD FOOTBALL TEAM HERE.
BEST IN THE STATE.
CENTERVILLE HIGH SCHOOL
BRRRRRRRRRRRRRNNNG!
WOW, THERE'S BUZZ! BEFORE WE GOT DIVORCED AND HE MUTATED INTO AN EVIL DOG! LOOK AT HIM--HE'S SO YOUNG AND HANDSOME...
COME ALONG, PATSY. WE'RE GOING TO BE LATE FOR CLASS.

HEY! THAT'S MY FRIEND HEDY!

HEDY! HEY!

BENEDICT ARNOLD MAY HAVE LED A CHARGE AT FREEMAN'S FARM DURING THE FIRST DAY OF WHAT BATTLE?

BREATHE IN... OUT... LET THE THOUGHTS DISSIPATE. REACH IN.
SEE IT.
Exam!

Exam!

THE BATTLE OF SARATOGA.

VERY GOOD.
HE'S ALSO HAVING AN AFFAIR WITH MRS. GRUNDELMAN.
NOW TRY TO MOVE THE APPLE ON HIS DESK.

WAPLSH

ALL RIGHT, WHO'S THE COMEDIAN?
BRRRRRNNNNNG

THIS IS EASIER THAN I REMEMBER.
HISTORY CLASS OR TELEKINESIS?
MISS WALKER!

HEDY TELLS ME YOU PULLED THAT LITTLE STUNT WITH MY RED DELICIOUS IN THERE!
BUT-- MR. BROWN, I--
PRINCIPAL'S OFFICE. NOW!

BETTER DO WHAT HE SAYS.

HEY, BUT...

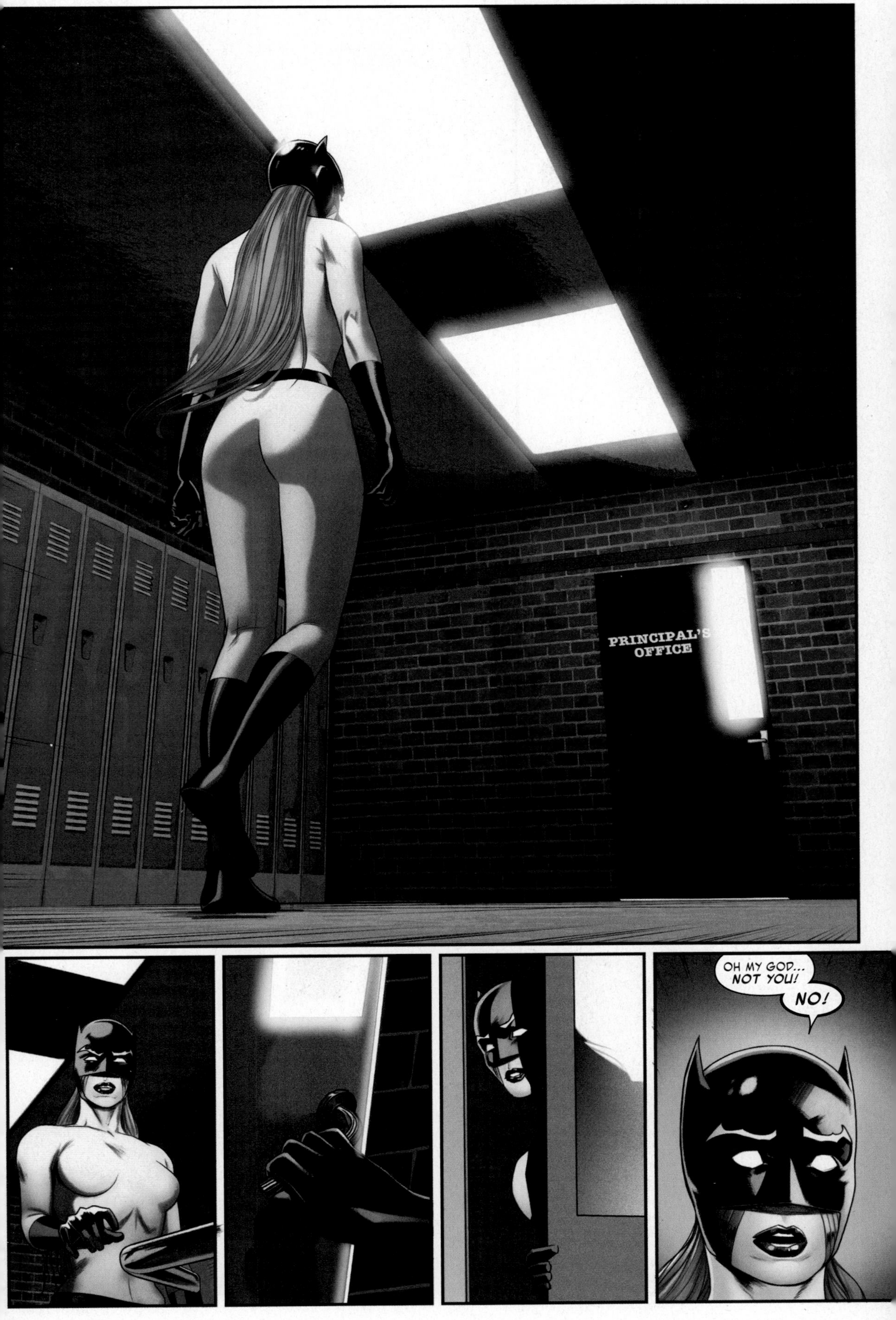

PRINCIPAL'S
OFFICE

OH MY GOD...
NOT YOU!
NO!

I MISS YOU SO MUCH... PATSY, I LOVE YOU...
I'M SORRY... PLEASE BE WITH ME AGAIN...
DAIMON HELLSTROM PRINCIPAL SON OF SATAN
NO! I WON'T GO BACK THERE! I CAN'T!
KCASTCHH!
YOU'RE BREAKING MY HEART, KITTEN...
DON'T BREAK MY HEART.
DON'T. BREAK. MY. HEART.
NOOOOOOO!

OH, MISS WALKER, IT'S JUST HORRIBLE THAT PATSY'S HAD A PSYCHOTIC BREAK AND BECOME TRAPPED IN HELL.
YES, HEDY, BUT HER COMPLETE BREAKDOWN IS MAKING FOR A WONDERFUL COMIC STRIP BOOK, RIGHT OUT OF THE GOLDEN AGE...

AND YOU'LL DRAW US AS BESTEST FRIENDS, RIGHT, MISS WALKER?
OF COURSE, HEDY.
AND NOT TO WORRY, BUZZ CAME BY WITH A NICE STRAIGHT RAZOR FOR PATSY THAT'LL FIX HER RIGHT UP.

OR WAS IT THAT HANDSOME DEMON BOY...?

REGARDLESS, I KNOW OUR PATSY WILL DO THE RIGHT THING AND OFF HERSELF SOON. SPARE US ALL THE TROUBLE OF ENDURING HER MISERABLE SUFFERING.

SHE IS WRETCHED FILTH NOW, YOU KNOW. CORRUPT AS SIN.
PERSONALLY, I THINK IT'S TOO MUCH TV.

LIGHTS OUT, SWEETIE.
I'M ON YOUR LAST PAGE.

...MOM?

NO... NO, PLEASE. I'M *BETTER* NOW...
MOM, TELL THEM I'M *BETTER NOW!*

NO FLAMES, NO TEETH! NO FLAMES, NO TEETH! *SEE?*
...SEE?

MOM... MOONDRAGON... *TONY...* *SOMEBODY...*

SOMEBODY!

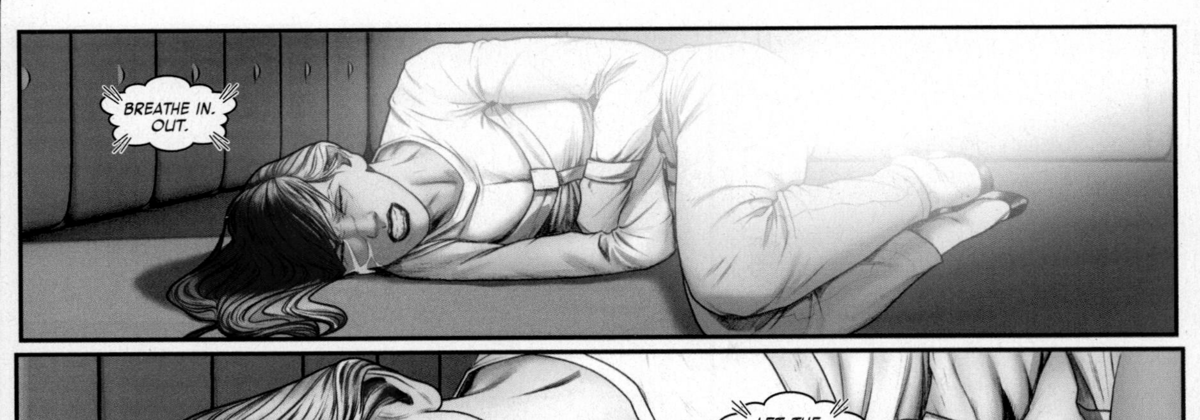
BREATHE IN.
OUT.

LET THE THOUGHTS DISSIPATE.

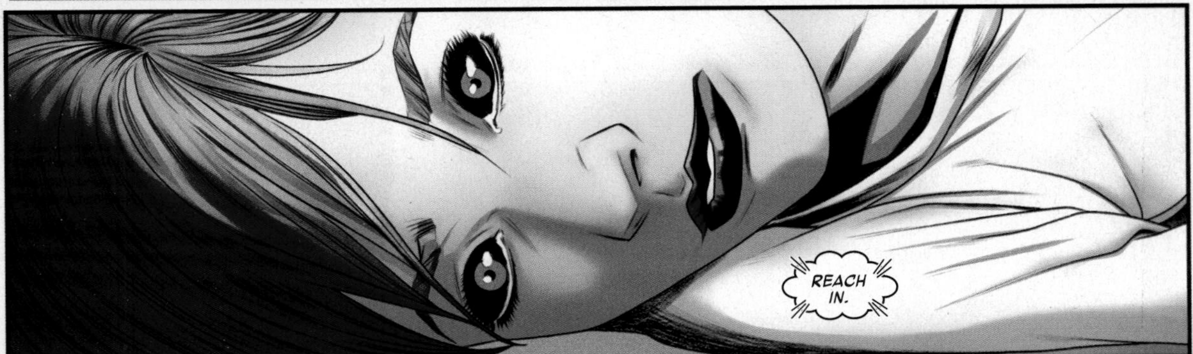
REACH IN.

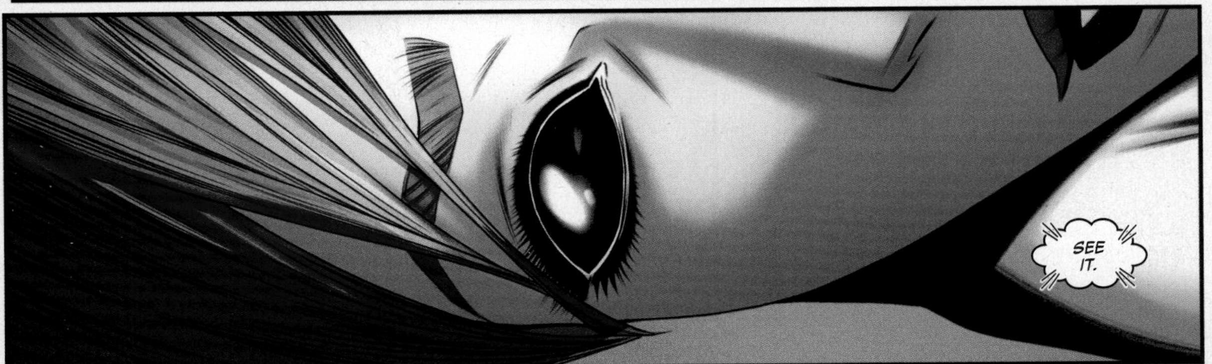
SEE IT.

WHO IS THAT?
YOUR FEAR.
FEAR OF YOUR OWN MIND.

WITH A SOFT TOUCH...

...FREE IT.

ACCEPT IT.

HOLD IT.

DEEP DOWN, KORVAC IS AFRAID.
IF YOU ARE NOT... YOU CAN WIN.

BEEP BEEP BEEP BEEP BEEP BE

EMERGENCY. EMERGENCY. IMMINENT HULL COMPRESSION.
EMERGENCY. EMERGENCY. REAR ENGINE 4 RUPTURE.

WHAT'S HAPPENING?!

THE #$%& IS *OFFICIALLY* HITTING THE FAN!

<WARNING: FIRE--CLASS C.> <ENGAGING.> <AUX.> FILTRATION... CHEMICAL. PRIORITY...? FINALIZED: CO. CO2. THE FOLLOWING TYPES OF HYDROCARBONS: <ALIPHATIC...>
I'M GONNA SLAM ON THE BRAKES AND SELF-DESTRUCT THIS OVERLOADED SPACE YACHT RIGHT IN THEIR FACES!
FIRE-SUPPRESSION SYSTEM DAMAGED. WARHEAD TEMPERATURES EXCEEDING SAFE ZONE.
TYPICAL STARK EQUIPMENT. ALL SHOW. NO GO.
UNICORN, FIRE ON MY MARK.
RHODEY, DON'T TOUCH THAT DIAL!
KADUNK
WE'RE OUTTA TIME!
GIMME TEN SECONDS, THEN THROW EVERYTHING TO THE ENGINES OR THE-- I DON'T KNOW--JUST MAKE IT GO AS FAST AS IT CAN!
THIS IS OUR ONLY CHANCE TO STOP THEM!
JUST DO IT, JAMES.

...AND F--
TRAITOR...
...LORD...?
COWARD...
YOU WILL ALWAYS BE OUR SLAVE, KORVAC.
KRRRSSHZZ!
ILLUSIONS, ALL!

WHOA! HUGE SURGE ON THEIR SHIP...

HE'S DROPPING OFF--
NOW!

ENGINE FOUR IS CONTAINED, AND THE SUPPRESSION SYSTEM IS BACK ONLINE!
CHNT

SUPPRESSANT FOAM--ENGAGED--
WAIT A MINUTE...
WHERE THE HELL IS TONY?

9

THE WILL OF FIRE

THE YEAR 2997.
WHAT DID YOU TELL THEM?
THE... LOCATION OF OUR RESISTANCE CELL...EVERYTHING. I'M SORRY, CAPTAIN, THE PAIN--
IT'S ALL RIGHT. THE THINGS THEY CAN DO... THE TORTURES... I'VE FELT IT, TOO.
SOMEONE'S COMING.
A GUARD?
I DON'T KNOW.
IT'S ME.
...MICHAEL?

KORVAC. THANK GOD.
WE GOT SEPARATED... CAPTURED. HOW DID YOU...? WE THOUGHT THE WORST--
NO TIME FOR THAT RIGHT NOW.
WE'VE GOT TO BREAK OUT OF HERE, GET WORD BACK TO EARTH. TELL THEM OF THE BADOON'S PLANS FOR INVASION.
NICE UNIFORM... WHERE'VE YOU BEEN HIDING THESE LAST FEW DAYS WHILE THEY PULLED US APART LOOKING FOR INTEL?
HYEOFFZ
HYEOFFZ
HYEOFFZ

IT'S DONE.
GOOD. THOSE EARTH-BORN WERE NO LONGER OF ANY USE.
THEY DIDN'T DOUBT MY INFILTRATION INTO THEIR REGIMENT FOR A SECOND.
YES, KORVAC, YOUR SKILLS IN BETRAYAL ARE PAR EXCELLENCE. TELL ME, HOW DOES IT FEEL TO BE A COWARD WHO TRADES THE LIVES OF HIS FELLOW SPECIES IN EXCHANGE FOR A MODEST POSITION WITHIN OUR EMPIRE?
RETURN TO YOUR STATION, EARTHBORN. TEND TO YOUR PRECIOUS COMPUTER MODULES AND DON'T WASTE MY TIME AGAIN.

WHAT IS THIS?!
YOU DARE LEAVE YOUR MODULE, YOU SNIVELING UPRIGHT WORM?! NO SLAVE ABANDONS HIS DUTIES!
I SHALL ENSURE YOU NEVER LEAVE THAT MODULE AGAIN!

NNYAAAAAAAA! AAAA! AAUUAAGGGHH!
NO... I BEG YOU...
NGGNGGNNNAAAAAAAA
MASTERS, PLEASE! I AM MORE THAN A MACHINE!
YOU'RE TOO WEAK, EVEN FOR A HUMAN!
SUFFER, SLAVE, AS METAL AND CIRCUITS MADE INCARNATE!
SERVE US AS NOTHING MORE THAN A SOULLESS MATRIX!
NOOOOOOOOO!

LORD KORVAC.
NOW.
WE'VE ARRIVED ON THE SURFACE OF THE RIVALIS MOON AND ARE READY TO DISEMBARK.
AND THE *ELECTROMAGNETIC SIGNATURE?*
JUST OVER 200 YARDS NORTHWEST.
"GOOD.
"I'M LOOKING FORWARD TO *MEETING* HIM."
THIS MOON'S ATMOSPHERE IS INCREDIBLY RICH IN OXYGEN.
THEN WE NEED TO BE EVEN *MORE* CAREFUL. CONTROLLER, BE READY, JUST IN CASE.
YES, LORD.
HERE, OTHER. JUST AS YOU DESCRIBED.
STAND BACK.

CHAAAOOOOOFFSH
I DON'T CARE WHO YOU ARE, YOU KNOW.
THERE CAME A TIME WHEN I WOULD HAVE. BUT NOT NOW.
THAT'S WHY I CHOSE THIS MOON AND THIS HOLE.
FWOOSHH
BECAUSE I WANT TO BE LEFT ALONE.
WAIT! THE UNIVERSE KNOWS YOU AS THE ORIGINAL Human Torch--
MY NAME IS JIM HAMMOND.

NO. YOUR NAME IS ADAM I.
WHO ARE YOU?
SOME ONCE KNEW ME AS KORVAC. BUT I WAS...REBORN. AND THE FIRST NAME GIVEN TO ME WHEN I AWOKE WAS ADAM IV.
I'M YOUR BROTHER.
GREAT, SO ANOTHER ANDROID, THEN.
MORE THAN THAT. A DIRECT EVOLUTION FROM THE SCIENCE OF PHINEAS HORTON, YOUR CREATOR, WITH ARTIFICIAL CELLS THAT EXACTLY MATCH YOUR OWN.
I'M NOT ADAM I ANYMORE. MY BODY WAS DESTROYED, REPLACED BY THIS GARBAGE SCRAP.*
*IN INVADERS #7. --TOM

RIGHT. THE WORK OF ONE TONY STARK. HIS SLAPDASH IGNORANCE CAN BE SPOTTED INSTANTLY.
LOOK, I DON'T KNOW WHAT YOU WANT, BUT I TOLD YOU WHAT I WANT. SO MAYBE GET LOST BEFORE I GET HOT UNDER THE COLLAR AGAIN.
HE MADE YOU A MONSTER. HE MADE YOU DEFICIENT, A MECHANICAL TOOL...
ALL RIGHT, NOW YOU'RE STARTING TO PISS ME OFF.
DON'T YOU WANT TO KNOW WHY I CAME ALL THIS WAY? WHY I TRAVELED LIGHT-YEARS TO FIND YOU?
JIM... I CAME TO MAKE YOU ADAM AGAIN.

I KNOW YOU WANT TO BE MORE THAN ONE OF TONY STARK'S BROKEN TOYS.
TRUTH IS, TONY MADE ME THIS WAY SO I COULD FIGHT AN OLD FRIEND.
A FRIEND WHO I GUESS WASN'T REALLY EVER MY FRIEND TO BEGIN WITH. BUT...A LONG TIME AGO, WE--

SO TONY USED YOU.
YOU HID YOURSELF AWAY HERE OUT OF SHAME.
TO PUT IT ONE WAY. AND NOW I DON'T EVEN HAVE... ME.

NO. I CAME HERE BECAUSE I FINALLY DECIDED #$%& EVERYBODY ELSE.

THE SAME THING HAPPENED TO ME ONCE. MY BODY WAS DESTROYED, GRAFTED TO MACHINE PARTS. IT WAS BRUTAL. TORTUROUS. CRUEL.
HOW DID YOU SOLVE YOUR PROBLEM?

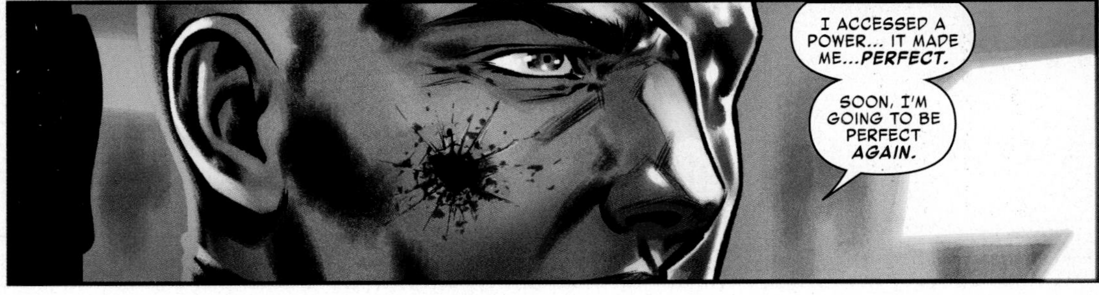
I ACCESSED A POWER... IT MADE ME...PERFECT.
SOON, I'M GOING TO BE PERFECT AGAIN.

AND I WANT YOU TO BE PERFECT WITH ME, JIM.
WELL, HEY, WE'RE JUST GETTING TO KNOW EACH OTHER.
I'M TALKING ABOUT GODHOOD.
I'M NOT INTERESTED IN BEING A GOD.
OF COURSE NOT. NEITHER AM I. I THINK OF IT AS A... MEANS TO AN END.
I ONLY NEED POWER IN ORDER TO SAVE EVERYONE ELSE. WHAT I REALLY WANT IS FOR THIS ENTIRE STRIFE-RIDDEN UNIVERSE TO BE AT PEACE. NO MORE WAR. NO MORE HATE. NO MORE FEAR.
NO MORE BETRAYAL.
HOW THE HECK ARE YOU GONNA PULL THAT OFF?
I'M GOING TO SHOW YOU, JIM.
BUT FIRST THINGS FIRST. I CAME HERE TO HELP YOU BECOME WHOLE AGAIN. DO YOU WANT MY HELP?
...YES.
I DO.

"I'M GOING TO RECONSTRUCT YOUR ANDROID FORM. HERE AND NOW.
"BUT I'VE IMPROVED IT. MODELED IT ON MY OWN, THE FOURTH ITERATION OF THE ADAM PROCESS.
"YOU WILL BE YOU AGAIN.
"BUT, AS A 'FREEBIE,' YOU'LL BE EVEN BETTER. STRONGER.
"THIS IS MY GIFT TO YOU, BROTHER."

WHY DO I DESERVE A GIFT LIKE THIS FROM YOU?
BECAUSE YOU'RE THE ONLY ONE ABLE TO FULLY SEE MY VISION FOR A BETTER EXISTENCE.
I CAN EXPLAIN IT TO LESSER BEINGS...TEACH IT, PROSELYTIZE IT...BUT YOU, ADAM I...YOU'LL BE ABLE TO ACTUALLY FEEL IT. IN ALL ITS LIVING GLORY.
IN YOUR UPGRADED ANDROID MIND I'LL IMPART SPECTERS OF MY OWN. THE KNOWLEDGE TO GRASP THE SCOPE OF MY MESSAGE. AND I'LL REVEAL TO YOU ITS ROOTS THAT GROW FROM MY PUREST HEART.
YOU WILL BE YOU, ADAM I. YOU'LL BE JIM HAMMOND. YOU WILL STILL BE THE TORCH. BUT YOU WILL SEE ALL AS IT IS MEANT TO BE, AND KNOW THAT IT'S UNDENIABLE.
AND AS FOR ME... I WILL NO LONGER BE ALONE WITH MY BURDEN OF SALVATION.
SHOW ME WHATEVER YOU WANT. I JUST WANT ARMS AND LEGS WHEN I SEE IT.
THE MENTAL AUGMENTATION WILL TAKE SOME TIME.
I WILL HAVE THE CONTINGENCIES READY.
I HAVE FAITH IN HIM. HE'LL SEE THE LIGHT.

"MICHAEL?

"MICHAEL? ARE YOU AWAKE?

I WILL BE THE COSMOS AND THE COSMOS WILL BE ME...

"MICHAEL, WAKE UP.

"I THINK YOU'RE HAVING A BAD DREAM..."

FOREST HILLS, NEW YORK. MANY YEARS AGO.

THESE DREAMS YOU HAVE... THEY'RE SO *AWFUL.* WHAT WAS IT THIS TIME?

JUST... THE PAST... ***STEALING*** THE POWER COSMIC...

NOT STEALING. ***CLAIMING.*** CLAIMING YOUR

I LOVE YOU, CARINA.
YOU'RE THE ONLY ONE WHO CAN REALLY SEE IT.
IF PEOPLE COULD JUST UNDERSTAND WHAT I'M TRYING TO DO, THEY WOULDN'T SEE ME AS A THREAT. THEY'D WANT TO HELP.
DNNG DONNG
MICHAEL KORVAC? ARE YOU IN THERE? WE NEED TO TALK...
BMM BM BMM
WE NEED YOU TO OPEN UP...
HEY THERE... SORRY TO BOTHER YA, BUT WE THINK SOMETHING IN THIS HOUSE MIGHT POSE GREAT PERIL TO THE FUTURE OF MANKIND.
YOU KNOW, THAT OL' CHESTNUT...

YOU CAN'T IMAGINE HOW VERY, VERY *SAD* THIS MAKES ME.

WHY'S THAT?
BECAUSE I WAS GOING TO BE YOUR *SAVIOR.*

BRING ALL OF EXISTENCE UNDER MY SANE AND BENEVOLENT RULE.

AH, THE HOPES...THE *DREAMS...*

IT'S *GONE* NOW, ALONG WITH MY SECRET...BUT... THOUGH I CAN NO LONGER SAVE THE *FUTURE--*
--I CAN SAVE MYSELF.

KKKZOOACK
AND THIS ONE, THE ONE CALLED IRON MAN, WHO WON'T GIVE UP!

I WIELD THE POWER COSMIC!
SPACTCH
NO! MICHAEL, YOU'RE KILLING THEM!
I'M... AWAKE...
MY BROTHER ADAM...CAN YOU SEE IT NOW?
FROM MY MIND TO YOURS, MY PLAN TO SAVE THIS UNIVERSE. TO GIVE IT ALL IT DESERVES...

I SEE...
OH MY GOD...
YES. ISN'T IT BEAUTIFUL? ISN'T IT PERFECT?
I SEE WHAT YOU DID...YOU... YOU KILLED THE AVENGERS.
YOU KILLED THEM ALL.
NO. IT WAS A MOMENT OF ANGER! I RESTORED THEM! I TOOK MY OWN LIFE INSTEAD! TO BUILD A NEW PLAN, A BETTER ONE THAT WOULD...
DAMMIT, JIM, I CANNOT BE OBSTRUCTED IN THIS WORK! I WON'T ALLOW IT!

YOU'RE SELFISH. YOU'VE ALWAYS BEEN SELFISH. THAT IMPRINT OF YOUR MIND YOU GAVE ME... IT'S SO OBVIOUS NOW THAT YOU'RE JUST A COWARD WITH DELUSIONS OF GRANDEUR!
BUT YOU, HOWEVER...A PATHETIC AND COMMON MANNEQUIN BLIND TO GREAT DESIGN, HINDERED BY MUNDANITY--
KZZK
THE CONTROL DISC IS CONFIGURED TO BLOCK ANY SELF-AWARENESS FROM THE ANDROID, AND ALL OF HIS SYSTEMS CAN NOW BE REMOTE CONTROLLED BY US.
VERY WELL.
LORD... HE WILL STILL PROVE A VALUABLE WEAPON AGAINST STARK AND HIS CADRE, AND WHATEVER ELSE WE MAY ENCOUNTER ABOARD TAA II.
I DIDN'T WANT A WEAPON, BASIL.
I WANTED AN ALLY. A BROTHER.
BUT I SUPPOSE I'LL CONTINUE TO REMAIN ALONE.
AND SETTLE FOR A SLAVE.

GOD, I FEEL HELPLESS.
I'VE BEEN STUCK HERE FOR SIX DAYS.
SIX EARTH DAYS, BY MY COUNT. DAYS HERE SEEM TO LAST FOREVER.

I STILL DON'T KNOW HOW I GOT HERE.
OR WHY I WAS BROUGHT HERE, IF THERE'S A REASON AT ALL.
I STILL HAVE NO IDEA HOW TO GET BACK TO WHERE I WAS BEFORE.

I NEED TO GET BACK TO MY TEAM. BACK TO PATSY, RHODEY.
AND I'M SURE KORVAC IS STILL OUT THERE, RACING TOWARD TAA II.
BUT LIKE I SAID, I'M HELPLESS. LIKE SOME CAST-ABOUT SCRAP METAL.

I COULD BE A BILLION LIGHT-YEARS FROM... WELL, FROM ANYTHING.
THERE WERE PEOPLE HERE ONCE. SOME KIND OF PEOPLE, A LONG TIME AGO. BUT THEY'RE GONE. DIED OFF.
BUT THERE ARE OTHERS HERE RIGHT NOW TOO. I'M NOT ALONE.

THE PEOPLE WHO ARE HERE ARE NOT FROM HERE EITHER.
I GUESS YOU COULD SAY THEY'RE ALL REFUGEES. LIKE ME.
AT A SINGULAR MOMENT IN THEIR LIVES, THEY EACH SUDDENLY FOUND THEMSELVES TRANSPORTED HERE WITH NO EXPLANATION. POWERLESS TO STOP IT.
THIS COLONY IS PRETTY STURDY, DESPITE EVERYONE BEING FROM DIFFERENT PARTS OF THE GALAXY OR, IN A FEW DISTINCT CASES, THE UNIVERSE.
NONE OF THEM KNOWS A WAY BACK TO WHERE THEY CAME FROM. AND SURPRISINGLY, MANY DON'T FEEL THE NEED TO TRY.
FOR SOME REASON, THEY LIKE IT HERE.
THEY'VE NAMED THIS PLACE MEGIDDO, AFTER THE CITY NEAR THE JEZREEL VALLEY IN ANCIENT GALILEE.
I'M GUESSING ONE OF THE HUMAN SETTLERS SUGGESTED IT.
AND I WONDER HOW MANY OF THE OTHERS KNOW THAT THE GREEK NAME FOR MEGIDDO IS ARMAGEDDON.
MAYBE--HOPEFULLY-- IT'S A JOKE.
BUT THE MEGIDDANS-- FOR LACK OF A BETTER WORD--HAVE EVEN OFFERED ME SHELTER AND A SHARE IN THE FOOD BANK.
GIVEN ME WATER TO DRINK AND BATHE IN.
IT'S ALL SPEARHEADED BY THE WOMAN IN CHARGE, YAR.

I'M ACTUALLY ASTONISHED BY THEIR AMOUNT OF TRUST. THEY ALL SEEM SO... HAPPY. AT PEACE, AT LEAST. WHY?
WE'VE ALL BEEN MAROONED HERE, BUT THEIR GRACIOUSNESS SUGGESTS THAT PEOPLE HAVE BEEN ARRIVING FOR SOME TIME AND THAT THEY'VE LEARNED TO RELY ON ONE ANOTHER.
WHAT THE HELL IS SO GREAT ABOUT THIS PLACE? IT'S A CHUNK OF BLUE DUST.
I EXPLAINED MY INJURIES. WHY I CAN'T TAKE MY HELMET OFF BECAUSE OF MY BROKEN NECK.
THEY'VE BEEN NOTHING BUT ACCOMMODATING. OVERLY SO.
IT'S NOT COMPLACENCY. IT'S LIKE THEY KNOW NONE OF US IS EVER GOING HOME.
THE PATROL IS JUST THAT. A DEFENSE OF WHAT THEY HAVE. IT FEELS MORE LIKE A MILITIA THAN ANYTHING ELSE. HELL, THEY'RE FRIENDS.
I DON'T EVEN GET ALONG WITH THE AVENGERS THIS WELL.

WEIRDEST THING IS, I KNOW ONE OF THEM. GUY NAMED COLIN RICHARD, GOES BY AVRO-X. MET HIM AT A ROBOTICS SYMPOSIUM IN LATVERIA AGES AGO.*
YOU STILL IN CANADA?
OH YEAH. WELL. I WAS, EH? TILL THIS.
*MARVEL FANFARE #44. --TOM

HOW LONG YOU BEEN HERE?
MORE THAN A YEAR, FOR SURE. BUT WE'RE DOIN' ALL RIGHT, ALL THINGS CONSIDERED.

YOU DON'T HAVE ANYBODY BACK HOME?
WE ALL DO, EH?
THAT'S TRUE.

WHAT IS OUT HERE, COLIN?
WELL, UH... YOU KNOW. IT'S NO CAKEWALK, FOR SURE...
WHAT'S NOT A CAKEWALK?

HAVEN'T YOU TALKED TO BIG MAN YET? BEST ASK HIM FIRST.
WHO'S BIG MAN? I THOUGHT YAR WAS IN CHARGE.
YAR MANAGES DAY-TO-DAY THINGS ON THE GROUND. BIG MAN IS... WELL, YA SEEN WIZARD OF OZ? HA... HE'LL CALL FOR YA SOON, DON'T WORRY...

HOW CAN THEY JUST GIVE UP? IT'S NOT IN MY BLOOD. I'M NOT GONNA LIVE SOME VERSION OF LITTLE HOUSE ON THE ALIEN PRAIRIE.
TRYING TO RESEARCH AN ESCAPE PLAN AT LEAST GIVES ME SOMETHING TO DO WHILE I WAIT ON THE WIZARD OF OZ.

I'VE ALSO FOUND ANOTHER PREOCCUPATION. A TROUBLING ONE.

GSSSN

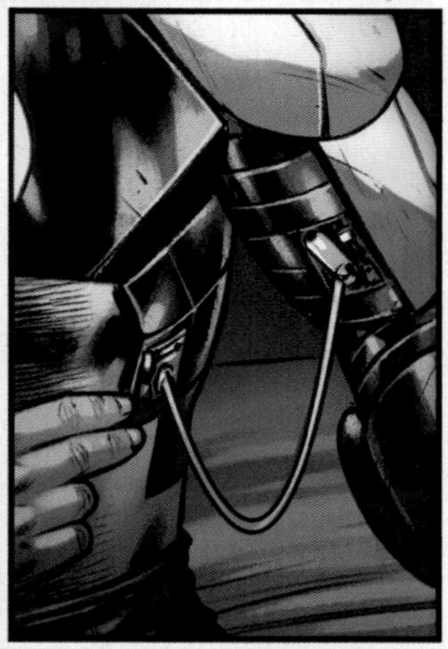

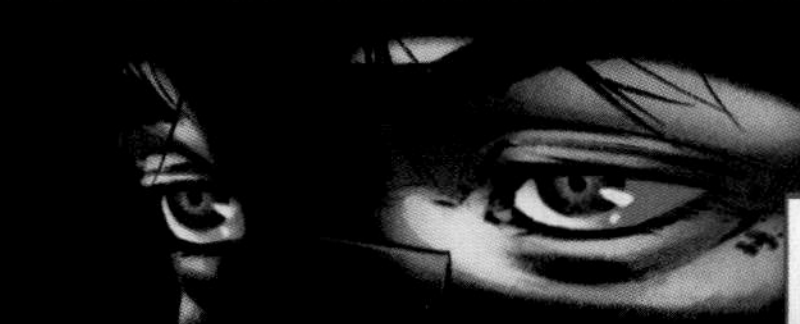
AFTER MY INJURY, I HAD HALCYON INSTALL A MORPHINE DRIP INTO THE SUIT. IT WAS SO I COULD CONTINUE TO FUNCTION AND NOT GO INTO SHOCK FROM PAIN.
RHODEY MADE FURTHER ADJUSTMENTS, MINIMIZING THE DOSAGE AND BUILDING IN A TIME-RELEASE TO MITIGATE AGAINST ADDICTION.

RHODEY KNOWS ABOUT MY... TENDENCIES. THIS WAS ONLY SUPPOSED TO BE AN EMERGENCY STOPGAP SOLUTION.
BUT IT'S BEEN SIX DAYS.
AND NOW I NEED IT. I CRAVE IT.
THE DRIP SYSTEM HAS ABOUT THREE MONTHS' WORTH OF DRUGS LEFT IN IT.
AND IT'S NOT LIKE I CAN'T HACK THE TIME-RELEASE.
THIS COULD GET REALLY, REALLY BAD.

STATCPH
CYBERNETICS. ANCIENT CYBERNETICS. WHAT THE HELL?
POWER. STILL STORED AND WARM. AND IT'S... DIFFERENT.
THERE'S... A LOT OF IT HERE.

EH. WHY NOT? I COULD USE A CHARGE.
GRRZZSH
IT'S NOT MORPHINE, BUT IT'S STILL SOMETHING PRETTY GOOD...
THE SUIT IS TAKING IT IN LIKE IT JUST FOUND A DESERT OASIS.

SEEMS LIKE WHATEVER THIS CIVILIZATION WAS, IT DISCOVERED A PARTICULARLY POTENT SOURCE OF ENERGY. IT'S...BIOLOGICAL. ENZYMATIC...

AND THEY MUST'VE DESTROYED THEMSELVES WITH IT.
IS THIS WHAT'S MAKING THE LOCALS GO GAGA FOR PLANET WHO-GIVES-A-#$%&?

AH YES, THE RUINS. QUITE A QUANDARY, AREN'T THEY?
A BIG ONE, YEAH...
THESE MACHINES WERE LIKELY BUILT BY THOSE WHO ULTIMATELY FAILED TO CONTROL THEM. WE USE THE POWER FOR OUR TURBINES AND GENERATORS.

HE'S READY TO SEE YOU, BY THE WAY.

I FEEL LIKE I WENT RIGHT TO THE WIZARD AND SOMEHOW SKIPPED THE WICKED WITCH OF THE WEST.
MAYBE I'M THE WITCH.
SOMETHING TELLS ME YOU'RE MORE THE GLINDA TYPE.
MUST BE MY PINK DRESS AND WAND.
I'LL BE DAMNED.
STILT-MAN?
HEY THERE, STARK.
OBVIOUS QUESTION, BUT WHAT ARE YOU DOING HERE?
HM. HARD ONE TO ANSWER.
MAKING DO, I GUESS.

SO WILBUR DAY IS THE MAN BEHIND THE CURTAIN?
DISAPPOINTED?
NO, JUST... CONFUSED.
ME TOO. FOR A LONG TIME I WAS, AT LEAST.

YOU'RE SNATCHING PEOPLE OUT OF THEIR LIVES AND DROPPING THEM ON THIS ROCK. WHY?
YOU'RE WRONG. I GOT HERE SAME AS YOU. I WAS ONE OF THE FIRST.
ONE BLINK OF AN EYE. THEN SOME NEW LONELY LIFE.
AND YOU RUN THIS PLACE. LEGITIMATELY.

WE'VE COME TO SEE LIVING HERE AS A GIFT.
SO HOW ARE YOU KEEPING A LEASH ON THESE FOLKS? THREATS? HYPNOTISM?

THERE'S NO SECRET. YAR'S THE PUBLIC FACE. A LOT OF PEOPLE OUT THERE KNOW ME BY DEED. I MAKE PEOPLE UNEASY IF I'M AROUND ALL THE TIME.
EVERYONE HERE LOST EVERYTHING. PEOPLE. PURPOSE. BUT ALSO...RESPONSIBILITIES. NOT JUST TO OTHERS, BUT ALSO TO SOME...VERSION OF OURSELVES WE BELIEVED NECESSARY.

IS THIS MAKING ANY SENSE?
I...
NOBODY HERE IS TRYING TO SAVE THE WORLD OR RULE IT. WE'RE JUST TRYING TO SUSTAIN SOMETHING TOGETHER.
LIKE A...WHAT, LIKE A HIPPIE COMMUNE?
WE COULD USE SOMEONE LIKE YOU.

NO, LET ME REPHRASE THAT. PERHAPS YOU COULD USE SOMETHING LIKE US.

I MEAN...I DON'T KNOW HOW TO... THANKS, I GUESS...
YOU KNOW HOW MANY TIMES YOU'VE TRIED TO KILL ME, WILBUR?
I DON'T KNOW WHAT THE STATUTE OF LIMITATIONS IS ON APOLOGIES, BUT I'M SORRY.

SO WHAT'S OUT THERE? WHAT ARE "THE ELEMENTS"?
I'LL ADMIT, IT'S SOMETHING PRETTY MONSTROUS. WE'VE NEVER BEEN ALONE HERE. THAT'S THE TRADE-OFF.
WE'VE BEEN ABLE TO REPEL IT EACH TIME, BUT WE ALWAYS LOSE SOME PEOPLE. PERHAPS WITH YOU, WE'LL STAND A REAL CHANCE.

NO OTHER DETAILS?
YOU'LL KNOW IT WHEN IT COMES. I DON'T WANT IT TO PREOCCUPY YOU. EXPERIENCE THE REST OF THIS PLACE FIRST.

WELL...IT'S WEIRD TO SAY, BUT...
I'M GLAD TO SEE YOU'RE DOING SO WELL OUT HERE.
THANKS.

"I'VE HAD A LOT OF TIME TO THINK."
WHAT IN THE LIVING HECK IS GOING ON? STILT-MAN IS SUDDENLY SOME REFORMED VERSION OF ALAN WATTS.
IT'S INTERESTING TO HEAR YOU BE SO ANXIOUS EVEN ON A HIGH DOSE OF MORPHINE.
HOW DO YOU KNOW ABOUT THAT?

STARK! LOOK ALIVE!
ARE THESE PEOPLE LIVING IN A DREAM?
HEY NOW! WHOOP-WHOOP!
LET'S SEE ONE, IRON MAN!
CRAK!
IS ANY OF THIS REAL?
GUY HITS A DOUBLE ON HIS FIRST AT BAT! MVP!
THAT'S RIGHT, CANADA!
IT'S REAL, TONY.

IT'S FUNNY TO HEAR YOU SAY IT'S REAL WHEN I CAN SEE THROUGH YOUR **ENTIRE BODY**. HOW ARE YOU EVEN **HERE**, PATSY?

IT'S PRETTY IMPRESSIVE. AND HERE I THOUGHT IT WAS JUST THE **MORPHINE**.

KORVAC'S BEEN PLAYING SO MANY MIND GAMES THAT MOONDRAGON FINALLY HELPED ME RE-UP MY ***MAD MENTAL SKILLS.***

ARE YOU BEING CAREFUL WITH THAT STUFF?

I'LL BE HONEST... IT'S GONNA BE A ***PROBLEM.*** *BUT ONE I'LL NEED TO DEAL WITH* ***AFTER*** *KORVAC. WHEN IT'S TIME...WILL* ***YOU*** *HELP ME?*

YOU ***KNOW*** I WILL.

BUT WE NEED YOU BACK HERE ***FIRST.*** *TAA II* IS ONLY A DAY AWAY TOPS.

I THINK THESE PEOPLE HERE NEED MY HELP TOO.

KORVAC WILL COME FOR ***EVERYTHING*** IN THE UNIVERSE. SEEMS LIKE THEY'D GET SWEPT UP IN THAT MESS AS WELL, RIGHT?

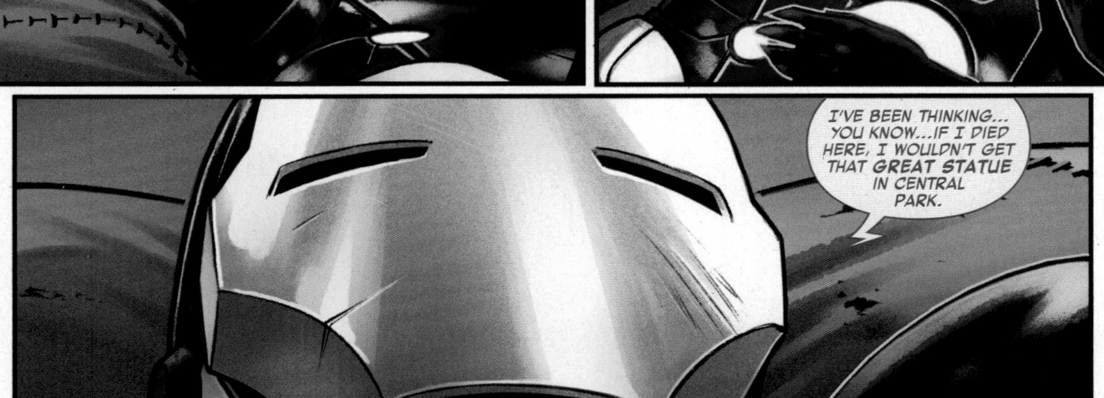

BOO-HOO.
NO, YOU'RE RIGHT. I MEAN... I THINK THAT WOULD BE FINE. BETTER. I COULD DO THE GOOD THING AND THAT WOULD BE THAT.
YOU MEAN DO IT WHILE NOBODY WAS WATCHING?
YEAH.

HERE I CAN... WAKE UP. HELP PLANT FOOD. BUILD THINGS PEOPLE CAN USE. AND IF THERE'S A PROBLEM, I JUST DEAL WITH IT.
BY THE WAY, DO YOU HAVE ANY IDEA WHERE "HERE" IS?
AS ENLIGHTENED AS YOU SOUND, I CAN'T FIGURE OUT YOUR ACTUAL LOCATION FOR THE LIFE OF ME. JUST REACHING YOU IS HARD ENOUGH.

I AM HARD TO REACH, AREN'T I? WHY IS THAT?
BECAUSE, BEFORE ANYTHING ELSE, YOU HAVE TO BE IRON MAN.
BUT HERE I'M JUST...

HERE YOU'RE JUST THE GUY THAT I KNEW WAS UNDERNEATH THIS ENTIRE TIME. THE SELFLESS ONE. A HERO. AND A FRIEND.

A HERO AND A FRIEND. I LIKE THAT.
THEN KEEP BEING IT. FOR THESE PEOPLE AND FOR THE REST OF THE UNIVERSE.

AND COME BACK TO ME, TONY STARK. I MISS YOU.
I MISS YOU TOO, PATSY WALKER...

WUBBOO
OOMMM
I WAS JUST COMING TO GET YOU!
WHAT'S GOING ON?
ATTACK ON THE PERIMETER.
BIG ONE?
ALWAYS IS, EH?
YAR AND MY PATROL ARE ALREADY TAKING UP POSITIONS ALONG THE TREE LINE, AND WILBUR IS INBOUND--
YOU GUYS EVER GONNA TELL ME WHAT THE HELL WE'RE ACTUALLY FACING?
WORDS DEFY. ANYWAY, IT'S **RIGHT** THERE, BUD...

ULTIMO?!
CORRECTION: AN ULTIMO. WE BELIEVE THIS MIGHT BE THE PLANET THEY ORIGINATED FROM CENTURIES AGO.
A PLANET OF ULTIMOS? ARE YOU KIDDING ME?!
KAK
TAACKKSHHH
WE JUST HAVE TO SCARE IT OFF. THEY'RE ACTUALLY MORE AFRAID OF US. WE'RE THE THREAT TO THEIR ENVIRONMENT.
YEAH, RIGHT, IT LOOKS REALLY SCARED...
"THE ELEMENTS"! I THOUGHT YOU MEANT, LIKE...A HEAVY THUNDERSTORM...
IT'S PART OF THE ECOSYSTEM, STARK! WE DIDN'T MAKE THE RULES!

IT STILL DOESN'T LOOK SCARED, GUYS...
BAEZZHHH
ZAARP!
TZCHAERT TZCHAERT
TZCHAERT
THIS ONE SEEMS REALLY RILED UP...
KRANGK
SPLATCHF
#$%&!
AH, GOOD GOSHDARNIT!
ROUNGK
TZCHAERT TZCHAERT
GET TO THE CAVERNS! NOW!

AND I WAS HAVING SUCH A NICE DAY...
I HEARD YOU PULLED JUICE OUT OF THE RUINS, EH? CAN YOU USE IT HERE?
I CAN'T CONCENTRATE SOMETHING LIKE THAT INTO A SINGLE BLAST WITHOUT BLOWING MY HANDS OFF.
WHAT ABOUT THAT THING IN YOUR CHEST? LAST TIME I SAW YOU, YOU WERE SHOOTIN' IT ALL OVER THE PLACE.
MY UNI-BEAM...?
WOW, I MEAN... IT'S BEEN A MINUTE SINCE I FIRED IT, AND THIS IS A NEW SET OF CLOTHES, BUT--
LET THEM GO!!!
KRAENGKCH
DO IT, YOU DAMNED ANIMAL!
GRNNNSKCH

OH MY GOD...
NO WONDER THE ENERGY IS ENZYMATIC. HE'S EATING THEM.
EATING US. CRIMINY, I NEVER GET USED TO IT...
YAR MIGHT'VE BOUGHT US SOME TIME. HE ATE HER RIFLE TOO--

ZZRAAOOK-PYAOTCHKA
FOOOOOOOOOM

HOLY... TONY... WE'VE ***NEVER*** KILLED ONE BEFORE.
COLIN'S RIGHT. THAT WAS... ***ASTONISHING.*** QUITE... ***ASTONISHING.***
THEY DERIVE THEIR POWER FROM **BIOMATTER.** I TOOK IN A **TON** OF IT OUT OF THE ANCIENT PIECES IN THE WILD EARLIER.

YAR, YOU GAVE SO *MUCH* OF YOURSELF TO THIS PLACE. OUR *HOME.* AND NOW YOU'VE GIVEN YOUR *LIFE* FOR IT.
AND WITH YOU GO *OTHERS* WHO ALSO CALLED THIS PLACE HOME. WE'LL MISS YOU. *EVERY ONE* OF YOU.

AVRO--COLIN. SORRY AGAIN THAT WE LOST 'EM...
IT'S OKAY, TONY. THEY *FOUGHT.* WE ALL DID. INCLUDING *YOU.*

"MELTED DOWN"...?
YOU ALL RIGHT, TONY?
ON EARTH, I UNDERSTOOD THE RULES. I'M IRON MAN. YOU'RE STILT-MAN. WE FIGHT.
BUT THIS PLACE IS...YA KNOW... DIFFERENT. PARADISE... KIND OF. STILL...I ALWAYS HAVE TROUBLE WITH INNOCENT PEOPLE GETTING KILLED...
I KNOW.

YOU'VE BUILT SOMETHING... AMAZING HERE, WILBUR. UNIQUE. SO WHY NOT TRY TO STAMP OUT THIS LAST TERRIBLE PART OF IT...ONCE AND FOR ALL?
I MEAN... "GREAT PLACE EXCEPT FOR KILLER ROBOTS" ISN'T A VERY GOOD TRAVEL BROCHURE, RIGHT...?

YOU THINK I HAVEN'T THOUGHT ABOUT THAT EVERY DAY?
BUT THE PEOPLE HERE, THEY'RE NOT LIKE YOU AND ME. WE'RE LUCKY TO EVEN HAVE AVRO-X. WE'RE REAL FIGHTERS. THEY'RE NOT.
AND I'M NOT GOING TO ASK THEM TO GO HEADLONG INTO BATTLE AND GET THEMSELVES KILLED. THE BEST I--WE--CAN DO... IS PROTECT THEM.
BUT, WILBUR, GOING AFTER THE ULTIMOS DOESN'T HAVE TO BE... PICKETT'S CHARGE. WITH THE RIGHT INFO, YOU COULD GO IN QUIET-LIKE AN' SHUT DOWN THE ENTIRE--
TONY. FROM WHAT COLIN AND I HAVE APPROXIMATED, THE SOURCE IS NOTHING SHORT OF A SINGULARITY. SELF-AUTOMATED. AN ENDLESS ASSEMBLY. BUT IT'S ALSO CONTINENTS AWAY.
EVEN IF ONE ERRANT MACHINE KNEW OUR EXACT LOCATION, IT WOULD TAKE MONTHS TO REACH US.
BUT THEY HAVE REACHED YOU. JUST LET ME HELP. I WANNA HELP...
I DO WANT YOUR HELP. BUT I THINK WE HAVE A BETTER CHANCE OF BEING RESCUED. I'VE BEEN WORKING ON A SIGNALING SYSTEM...
TOTALLY...THAT MAKES SENSE... BUT ALSO... THIS IS...
IT'S A BEAUTIFUL HOME WE'VE CREATED, YES. EVEN IF BY ACCIDENT.
IT'S FUNNY, IN A WAY. I THINK THE THREAT OF THE MACHINES IS WHAT KEEPS THE COMMUNITY BOUND TOGETHER. NO DISSENT.
STILL, WILBUR... KILLER ROBOTS, MAN. WITHOUT THOSE, THIS PLACE COULD...GROW. BUILD ON THE GREAT IDEAS YOU'VE ALL DISCOVERED.

TONY, I'M SINCERELY ASKING FOR YOUR HELP WITH THE RESCUE SIGNAL. I BET WE COULD HAVE IT WORKING WITHIN WEEKS, IF NOT DAYS.
I... OF COURSE. YEAH...
LET'S JOIN THE OTHERS FOR DINNER. WE CAN KEEP TALKING.

STILT-MAN...
I CAN'T TELL YOU HOW LITTLE MY LIFE MAKES SENSE TO ME THESE DAYS...
IRON MAN.
SEEMS LIKE ONLY YESTERDAY DAREDEVIL WAS PILE-DRIVING ME THROUGH A PARKED CAR.* BUT TONIGHT... IT'S BUTTERNUT SQUASH AND WHAT I CAN ONLY DESCRIBE AS "BIRD-MEAT STEW."
*DAREDEVIL #20. --TOM

EXCUSE ME. AREN'T YOU FORGETTING SOMETHING?
...PATSY...?
YOU GOT IT, PAL--THIS IS HELLCAT CALLING ON THE MIND PHONE. CAN I STEAL YOU AWAY FROM THE BIRD-MEAT STEW FOR A SECOND?

G'ON AHEAD. I'LL BE IN SOON...
SO, WHAT, YOU'RE BEST BUDS WITH STILT-MAN NOW?

HEY, STOP--ARE YOU READING MY MIND?
JUST TRYING TO GET UP TO SPEED ON WHAT THE HECK YOU'RE DOING.
DON'T DO THAT, PATSY-- IT'S RUDE. AN' IF YOU REALLY WANT TO TALK, LET'S... GO SOMEWHERE ELSE.

YOU KNOW, EVEN WHEN YOU'RE LIKE THAT... ALL...GLOWY... YOU LOOK GREAT--
I KNOW--I'M SORRY. I GOT CAUGHT UP IN... THE PEOPLE HERE, THEY REALLY... NEED MY HELP.
ONE WORD, TONY-- KORVAC.
THESE PEOPLE FROM THIS PLANET YOU'RE ON--DO THEY EXIST IN THE KNOWN UNIVERSE?
YEAH. AT LEAST I THINK SO...
THEN MAYBE YOU CAN HELP THEM BY STOPPING KORVAC BEFORE HE HORRIFICALLY TRANSMOGRIFIES SAID KNOWN UNIVERSE.
LOOK, I DON'T EVEN KNOW WHERE I AM--
I KNOW YOU DON'T KNOW THAT--
STOP WITH THE MIND READING! THIS PLACE, IT'S...WELL, IT'S SO...
PERFECT?
YES.
EXCEPT FOR THE ULTIMO MACHINES THAT EAT PEOPLE.
PATSY, C'MON--
TONY, I KNOW YOU'VE TURNED OFF YOUR MORPHINE GOVERNOR. SO LET'S GET REAL.
HOW HIGH ARE YOU RIGHT NOW?

...I'M SORRY.
AND MY ANSWER IS... VERY.
YOU'VE BEEN CARRYING A LOT ON YOUR SHOULDERS. BUT THE THING IS...YOU DON'T HAVE TO. NOT ALONE. YOU HAVEN'T FIGURED THAT OUT YET, HAVE YOU?
THE REST OF US HAVE DECIDED TO FACE KORVAC ON TAA II WITHOUT YOU.
WHAT ARE YOU SAYING?
NO. PLEASE DON'T. YOU HAVE TO WAIT FOR ME.
WE HAVE A VISUAL. WE MANAGED TO BEAT KORVAC HERE, AND WE CAN'T MISS THE CHANCE TO GET THE JUMP ON HIM WHEN HE SHOWS UP.
ALL YOUR DEATHS COULD END UP ON MY CONSCIENCE. IT'LL BE ALL MY FAULT.
STOP DOING THAT. WHEN YOU SAY IT'S ALL YOUR FAULT, YOU MAKE IT ABOUT YOU. YOU TAKE AWAY EVERYBODY ELSE'S CHOICES. WE'RE NOT REFLECTIONS OF YOU.
WE'RE TRYING TO BE HEROES. AND OUR EXECUTIVE DECISION IS TO TAKE ON KORVAC ALONE IF WE HAVE TO.

TAKE CARE OF YOURSELF, TONY. ONCE WE GET THROUGH THIS, WE'LL COME FIND YOU.
AND TURN YOUR MEDICINE GOVERNOR BACK ON BEFORE WE ALL LOSE YOU PERMANENTLY.
WE'RE ANCHORED TWO HUNDRED KLICKS OUT FROM THE WORLDSHIP. SO WHAT'S THE NEXT MOVE?
WE'RE ON OUR OWN.
THIS ALREADY FELT LIKE A SUICIDE MISSION...
WE HAVE NO IDEA WHERE HE IS? NO WAY TO GET HIM?
EVEN IF WE COULD... HE'S IN NO SHAPE TO DO THIS. TRUST ME.
IT'S JUST US. SO, I GUESS LET'S TRY TO SAVE THE UNIVERSE.

I TOLD YOU THIS ULTIMO WRECK WAS OFF-LIMITS, TONY.
MAY I ASK WHY IT'S OFF-LIMITS? DO YOU EVEN KNOW WHY IT'S OFF-LIMITS?
WILBUR'S BEEN THROUGH A HALF-DOZEN OF THESE THINGS, EH? IT'S A WASTE OF TIME OTHER THAN THE POWER STORAGE.
AH, SO IT'S WILBUR WHO SAYS IT'S OFF-LIMITS--
WEET-
CHOOWWW

YOU'RE NOT IN CHARGE OF THIS COLONY, TONY.
YOU'RE NOT IN CHARGE OF ANYTHING.
OKAY, WELL, I'M GONNA HAVE TO PULL MY PUNCHES BECAUSE OTHERWISE I'LL KILL YOU.
GOTTA GET CLOSE ENOUGH, EH?
WHSSSHHHHHH
AGK!
WHAT ARE YOU PROTECTING?
WNNNNGCH
WHAT ARE YOU HIDING?
CRNGSCH

I KNOW THESE THINGS ARE DANGEROUS ENOUGH THAT WE DON'T WANT ANYONE MESSING WITH THEM...
"WE"? YOU AND WILBUR?
I DO WHAT HE SAYS. HE OVERSEES THE COLONY, HE KEEPS IT GOING...

WHAT ELSE DOES HE TELL YOU TO DO?
JUST-- PROTECT THIS PLACE! NOT LET... ANYTHING--ANYONE-- UPSET THE BALANCE!

UPSET THE BALANCE?
HE SAID... IT'S... FRAGILE...

WRENCH

FIND SOMETHING...?
I'M NOT THAT FAMILIAR WITH COMPUTERS BUILT BEYOND THE LAST MILLENNIUM...BUT THIS ONE HAS AN I.R. REMOTE CONTROL CIRCUIT GRAFTED TO IT. SILICON CHIPS, TIN SOLDER...

"VERY RECENT WORK."
PZSEEEW PCHFFFFFSH
TONY, COLIN... DID YOU TRY KNOCKING FIRST? MAYBE I WAS DISTRACTED AND DIDN'T HEAR IT.
I'VE BEEN DOING SOME BETA TESTS ON THE RESCUE SIGNAL.
LIKE HELL YOU ARE.
THE ULTIMOS. THEY'RE BEING CONTROLLED REMOTELY.
LIKELY BY THE SINGULARITY THAT'S BUILDING THEM--
A SENTIENT SINGULARITY DOESN'T SHOP AT RADIO-SHACK.
ARE YOU ACCUSING ME OF SOMETHING?
YEAH. MURDER.

THIS IS MY HOME, TONY. AND I'M STARTING TO THINK YOU SHOULD LEAVE.
RIGHT. PERHAPS HORIZONTALLY, LIKE THE OTHER COLONISTS WHO'VE GOTTEN IN THE WAY.
HOW COULD YOU DO THIS TO US? WE TRUSTED YOU!
NEITHER OF YOU UNDERSTAND A DAMN THING, DO YOU?
THE ULTIMOS-- THEY'RE PART OF THE ECOSYSTEM. JUST LIKE EVERYTHING ELSE HERE.
WHAT DO YOU MEAN? PROTECTED LIKE WILDLIFE? BECAUSE THEY'RE NOT EXACTLY GAZELLES.
GOOD GOD, STARK, OPEN YOUR EYES TO THE GRAND EXPERIMENT. THE EXPERIMENT THAT'S WORKING.

KNNNNSSNKCH
I'D HAD ENOUGH OF EVERYTHING BACK HOME. BEING CONSTANTLY HUMILIATED WHEN ALL I WANTED WAS A STAKE IN SOMETHING.
SO I CAME HERE WITH A PLAN. I WANTED TO SHOW THAT I COULD BE A LEADER. CREATE SOMETHING GOOD. AND I DID.
YOUR LITTLE... TERRARIUM...HAS... SOME FLAWS...
NOT FLAWS. BALANCE. THE INTERFERENCE BEAM BROUGHT YOU ALL HERE ONE BY ONE. I JUST PRETENDED AS IF THE SAME THING HAD HAPPENED TO ME. THAT WAY WE WERE ALL IN IT TOGETHER. FIGHTING FOR SURVIVAL. BONDING.
YOU... BROUGHT US HERE...?
OF COURSE, COLIN. AND I GAVE YOU WHAT YOU ALL WANTED. SOMEWHERE THAT WAS JUST YOUR OWN. WHERE YOU COULD LET GO OF WHAT YOU WERE BEFORE. LIVE NOW, WITH OTHERS.

QUEAESTCHKCH
THEN WHY THE ULTIMOS? WHY KILL OFF YOUR LOYAL SUBJECTS?
CLTNK
KCHNK
THE ONES WHO LIVED HERE BEFORE, THEY CREATED THE ULTIMOS. THE ULTIMOS DESTROYED THEM. ROAMED FREE. BUT I LEARNED HOW TO REPROGRAM THEM.
ZREEOF ZREEOF ZREEOF
ITSCHK!

AAAGH!
CREYOONKCK
KNNNFFF
WHY REPROGRAM THEM? WHY USE THEM TO KILL?
BECAUSE...

...I COULDN'T...LET THE COLONY GROW TOO BIG... I MIGHT LOSE LEADERSHIP... CONTROL. SO I KEPT IT SMALL...
...AND WITH... A THREAT...ALWAYS LOOMING...THERE'D BE NO... INFIGHTING...ARGUING... FACTIONS... ANY OF IT...
JUST...PEACE... HAPPINESS.

WHEN I HEARD THE S.O.S. SIGNAL FROM YOUR SHIP...I HAD TO BRING YOU, TONY... IT WAS RISKY, BUT I HAD TO SHOW YOU... THAT I COULD...LEAD...SOMETHING... PURE.
IT'S NOT PURE, WILBUR. IT'S SICK. AND SAD.

AND...FROM WHAT IT LOOKS LIKE... PRETTY DANG INFURIATING.

NO. DON'T DO THIS.
LET'S ALL REMAIN CALM--

YYYYAAAAAAAAHHHH!

PLEASE! NO!

I LOVE YOU ALL! I LOVE ALL OF YOU!
COLIN, WHAT IF THEY--?
THIS IS A SOCIETY AND THEIR INJUSTICE. YOU HAVE TO TRUST THEM TO DEAL WITH IT HOW THEY BEST SEE FIT.

I WON'T LET THEM KILL HIM.
THESE ARE **GOOD PEOPLE**. THERE'S ALREADY BEEN **TOO MUCH** DEATH. THEY **KNOW** THAT.

FLEEAAZSSZHOOO
HOLY GEEZ--

TONY STARK.

OH BOY.
I DIDN'T REALIZE THE **LIVING TRIBUNAL** KNEW MY FULL NAME... SEEMS **BAD**...

THE UNIVERSE IS ON THE VERGE OF CATASTROPHIC IMBALANCE. ONLY YOU CAN RESTORE THIS BALANCE. YOU MUST TRAVEL TO THE WORLDSHIP OF GALACTUS AT THIS VERY MOMENT.

RIGHT, YEAH, KORVAC. HE'S TALKING ABOUT THIS ANDROID NAMED KORVAC--WHO WANTS THE POWER COSMIC--
ANYWAY, IT LOOKS LIKE I'VE GOTTA GO...

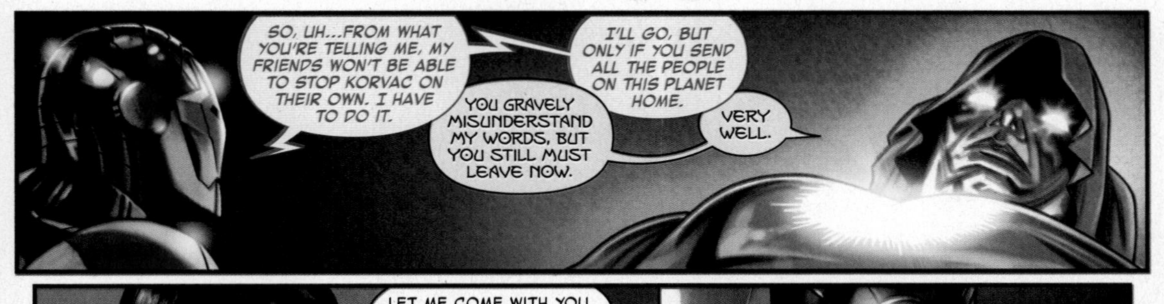

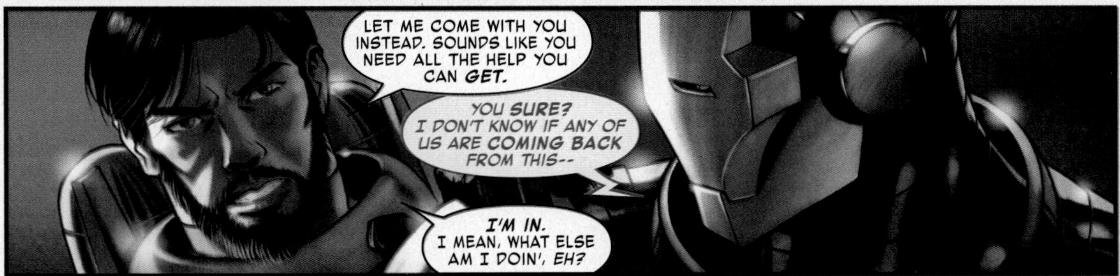

FLEEAAZSSZHOOO

...WAS THAT IT?
ARE WE ON TAA-II?
JUDGING BY THE SIZE OF THIS PLACE...I'D SAY YES.
AND...LUCKY US, PERHAPS...I THINK WE'RE ENTIRELY ALONE... NO KORVAC. AND NO FLYING PURPLE PLANET-EATER...

INTRUDER ALERT. INTRUDER ALERT.

BUT I THINK WE JUST ACTIVATED HIS DEFENSE SYSTEMS...

TO BE CONTINUED!

MARVEL
$3.99
WOMEN'S HISTORY
PATSY WALKER
EST. 1944
JEN BAR TEL

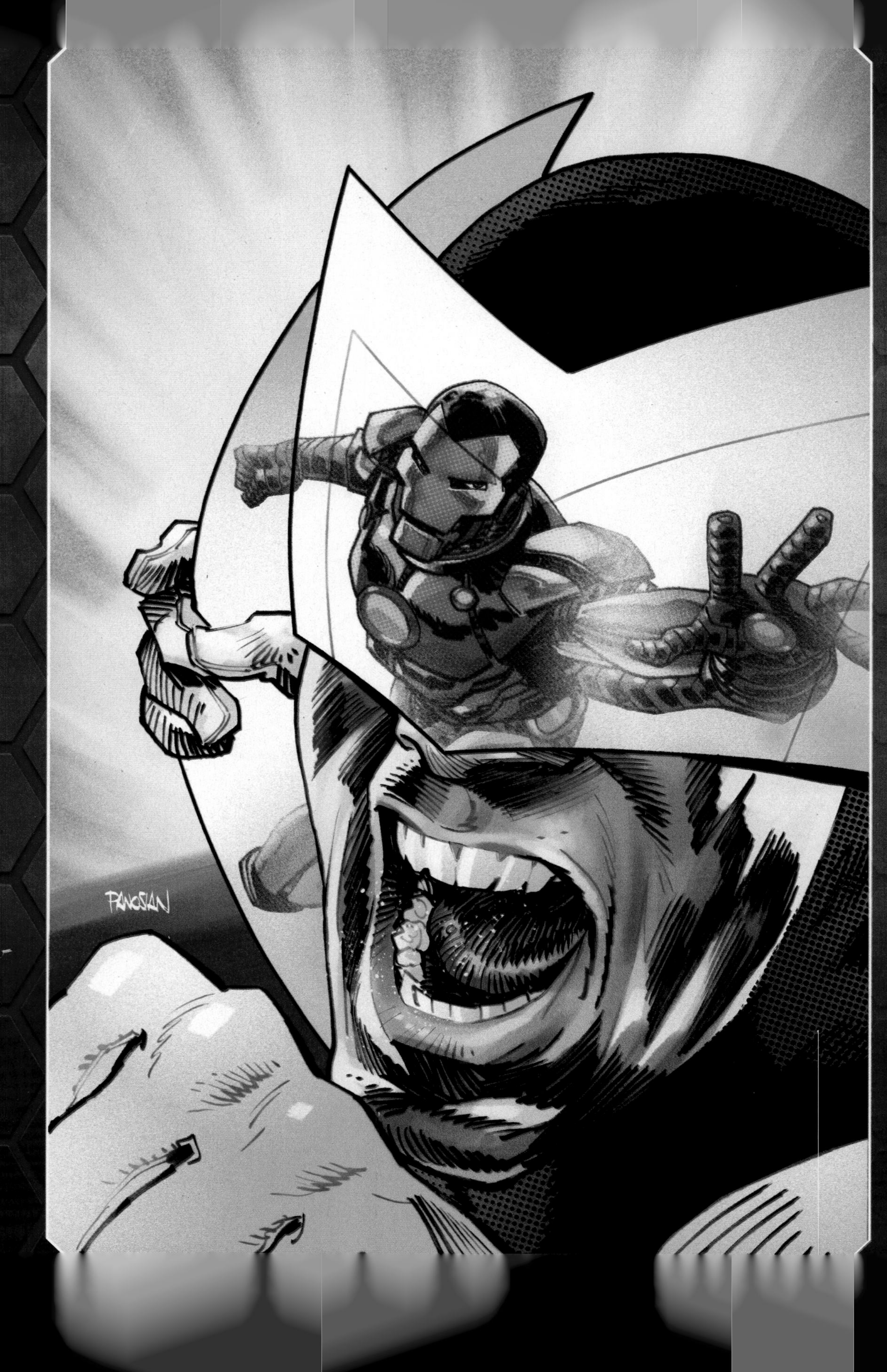
PANOSIAN

JOHN CASSADAY & DAVE STEWART
10 CAPTAIN AMERICA 80TH ANNIVERSARY VARIANT

FOURTH EDITION

STRAIGHT TALK *about* BREAST CANCER

FROM DIAGNOSIS TO RECOVERY

SUZANNE W. BRADDOCK, M.D.
JANE M. KERCHER, M.D.
JOHN J. EDNEY, M.D.
MELANIE MORRISSEY CLARK

Addicus Books
Omaha, Nebraska

An Addicus Nonfiction Book

Fourth Edition
ISBN: 978-1886039-97-1

Cover design by Peri Poloni-Gabriel
Illustrations by Jack Kusler

This book is not intended to serve as a substitute for a physician. Nor is it the authors' intent to give medical advice contrary to that of an attending physician.

All proceeds from the sale of this book are donated to the Straight Talk about Breast Cancer Charitable Trust and are used to assist breast cancer patients and their families.

Library of Congress Cataloging-in-Publication Data

Straight talk about breast cancer : from diagnosis to recovery / Suzanne W. Braddock ... [et al]. — 4th ed.
p. cm.
Includes index.
ISBN 978-1886039-97-1 (alk. paper)
1. Breast—Cancer—Popular works. I. Braddock, Suzanne W., 1942-

RC280.B8S748 2007
616.99'449—dc22 2006031408

Addicus Books, Inc.
P.O. Box 45327
Omaha, Nebraska 68145
AddicusBooks.com

Printed in the United States of America

To the memory of
Debra T. Hartmann, who was instrumental in
making this book available to many women
while serving as program manager
for the Nebraska "Every Woman Matters" Program

Contents

Preface

Please read this book imagining that a very good friend is sitting close to you, giving you this introduction to the rest of your life with love and understanding. Imagine your friend—who has indeed walked in your shoes—taking you by the hand and guiding you through the next few weeks.

Your friend wants to help you understand what is happening, and help you cope with the decisions and treatments ahead. She also wants to help your family and friends, for they are suffering with you.

Know there will come a time when you'll go entire minutes without thinking of breast cancer—then hours, and even days. Of course, your life will never be the same. In fact, it will probably be better in many ways you would not have chosen but will be delighted to discover.

The authors of this book reach out to you as dear friends and offer you the hope of a complete recovery, along with the certainty that the journey from here will be one of growth, challenge, and change. That is, after all, what life is about.

Acknowledgments

We, the authors, would like to thank those who helped make this book possible. We are grateful to physicians Margaret Block, M.D., Robert Langdon Jr., M.D., Patrick McKenna, M.D., Janalyn Prows, M.D., Henry Lynch, M.D., Ramon Fusaro, M.D., John J. Heieck, M.D., Richard Bruneteau, M.D., and Carol Kornhehl, M.D., author of *The Best News about Radiation Therapy.*

We thank Mollie Foster, Ph.D., for her contributions and Judy Dierkhising, Ph.D., for her insights into the emotional needs of breast cancer patients. Our appreciation goes to the Nebraska Methodist Hospital Breast Cancer Support Group for their comments, wit, and strength. And with gratitude, we remember Sue Kocsis, a real spark, whose encouragement meant so much during the early stages of this book.

We are also deeply grateful to the women who shared their personal stories in order to help others. A special thanks to the women who shared their surgery and reconstruction photos. We acknowledge photographers Larry Ferguson and Paula Friedland for their creativity and sensitivity in portraying these women as real, living people, rather than medical subjects. We thank Jack Kusler, who provided illustrations for the book.

Introduction

Someone you love or someone you know will get breast cancer—your friend, your aunt, your mother, your father, your daughter, yourself. The fact is, if you are an American woman, your chance of getting breast cancer is especially high—about one in eight over your lifetime. Last year in the United States, nearly 200,000 women were diagnosed with breast cancer.

Here's the good news: Thanks to early detection and better ways to treat breast cancer, more and more women with breast cancer are surviving. The percentage has climbed steadily since 1989—not just five-year disease-free survival, either, but real, lasting, bounce-the-grandkids-on-your-knee survival.

The rest of my life started April 1, 1992, with a phone call from my friend and doctor, who informed me that the lump in my breast was malignant. I reacted, as do most women, with the irrational certainty that I was going to die, and soon. I was 49.

Although I am a physician—a dermatologist—I knew little more about breast cancer than what I had learned in medical school in the late 1970s. Back then, I saw several patients who died from the disease, and I was afraid. So I started doing the "right things." I dutifully saw my physician every year for an exam (right). I had a baseline mammogram between ages 35 and 40 (right) and a mammogram every other year between 40 and 50 (right). I began planning for annual mammograms when I was about to turn 50 (right—though experts now recommend annual mammograms after 40). I also practiced breast self-examination on a "regularly sporadic" basis (wrong). Like many women, I had "lumpy" breasts, making self-examination difficult to interpret. I relied on my physicians and mammograms to keep me safe (very wrong).

When I learned that I had breast cancer, I was disappointed that three doctors who had examined me many times had failed to recommend a biopsy—a test that takes a tissue sample and analyzes it for cancer. I was disheartened that mammograms had failed to detect my cancer. But more than anything, I was amazed at myself—that I had been so cavalier about the very precautions that could have diagnosed my tumor sooner: doing monthly breast self-exams without fail, and insisting on further tests on a lump that worried me. Denial is a powerful thing.

Fortunately, my cancer had not yet spread when it was diagnosed, at least not that the existing technology could determine. The tumor was medium-size—2.2 centimeters, a little under an inch, in diameter.

Surgery is almost always recommended for breast cancer. I chose to have a mastectomy—surgery to remove the breast—followed by chemotherapy. Women with breast cancer are offered chemotherapy when their tumors are of a certain size or they are in a high-risk category for recurrence. "Adjuvant treatments" such as chemotherapy and drugs such as Herceptin can prevent or postpone a recurrence of the cancer and improve the chance of long-term survival.

The usual chemotherapy for early-stage breast cancer, while no picnic, is no longer the ordeal it used to be. Now there are drugs to help with nausea and fatigue, and to stimulate blood-cell production in the bone marrow—thereby helping to prevent infection and possibly detrimental treatment delays.

Of course, chemotherapy has turned wig-making into a real growth industry. Your bad-hair day lasts about nine months. My daughter, Gail, had a lot of fun playing with my wig—or, as we called it, "the muskrat." Actually, I learned to appreciate the ease with which I could wash my "hair"—swish it in a bowl of suds, rinse it, and hang it to dry. I also enjoyed snatching it off at stop lights on the hot drive home from work and chuckling at other drivers' startled expressions.

Going through surgery and chemotherapy mobilized me, and it was easy to focus on milestones: one-third done, halfway done—finished! My eyelashes returned, and before I knew it, I was ready to donate the muskrat to the American Cancer Society's wig bank. I could climb the hill behind my house without gasping for breath, and finally, I went an entire day without thinking about breast cancer.

My days now, since chemotherapy, are as precious as the glimpse of a small garden behind a city brownstone. These are good days. They have shown me, in a poignant and powerful way, that life is best lived by us all, with or without cancer, in a state of radical trust. Trust, and trust, and trust some more. None of us knows the limits of our days, but we do know Who limits them. And that is all we need to know.

—Suzanne Braddock, M.D.

Wind

I sit silent in the cold room, reading,
when softly, a stir outside calls me away. It is the wind,
moving the frozen oaks and evergreens, pushing the
snow across the ice on the lake.
It is a sound both great and small,
the breath of God over the land
the voice of creation,
giving life to this cold, barren landscape,
to my days of terror.
I feel the power embraced in that sound,
and joy in the force that is greater than I,
greater than cancer, greater than all the pain in all the women.

—Suzanne W. Braddock, M.D.

1

Understanding Breast Cancer

You might think the phrases "good news" and "breast cancer" don't belong in the same sentence—or even the same zip code. And in one way, you'd be right: A diagnosis of breast cancer is never good news.

But amazing things are happening in breast cancer prevention, diagnosis, and treatment, and the good news just keeps getting better. For example, since 1989, the death rate from this disease has declined more than 2 percent a year, even though the number of cases has gradually risen. Nearly 200,000 women are diagnosed with breast cancer in the U.S. each year. And the majority of women whose breast cancer is discovered early are cured.

Partly because of a surge in breast cancer publicity, more and more women are learning about this illness and about their own level of risk. The more they know, the more faithfully they practice self-examination, schedule mammograms, and take care of their health. In turn, more cases of breast cancer are detected early and the survival rate continues to rise.

You can see why every woman, regardless of her age, needs information about breast cancer—especially in the United States, where the breast-cancer rate is among the highest in the world. If you have breast cancer, knowledge is the most potent antidote to fear and the best preparation for treatment. If you do not have breast cancer, knowledge is your strongest protection.

The best way to start learning about breast cancer is with an understanding of the healthy breast.

Breast Structure and Function

The human female breast is so glamorized and commercialized in our culture, it's easy to forget that the breast has a serious job—producing milk for babies. Even a quick look at breast structure reminds us of this important function.

The breast is made up of fatty tissue that contains blood vessels and lymph vessels, plus fifteen to twenty rounded divisions called *lobes*, themselves formed of dozens of smaller *lobules* that end in tiny *bulbs*. The lobular system produces milk in response to hormonal changes after childbirth or after an abortion or a late miscarriage. Milk flows from the lobes and bulbs through narrow tubes, or *ducts*, leading to the *nipple*, which protrudes from the center of the *areola*—the circle of darker skin at the tip of the breast.

Lymph vessels in the breast carry *lymph*, a pale fluid containing white blood cells, to *lymph nodes*—small, rounded masses of tissue that act as filters for this fluid. Lymph serves to transport infection-fighting cells to all parts of the body.

Breast cancer isn't a death sentence. We've made so much progress in the last 20 years. In the future, I believe breast cancer will be viewed more as a chronic disease, like hypertension or diabetes.
—Kathryn, oncology RN

There are lymph vessels and nodes throughout the body, but the lymph nodes nearest to the breast are *usually* the first ones affected when breast cancer begins to spread. In a discussion of lymph nodes, you may hear the terms *sentinel node* and *axillary nodes*. The sentinel node is the first lymph node that lymph fluid reaches in the under arm area after leaving the breast. Axillary nodes refer to any of the lymph glands in the armpit.

What Is Cancer?

Every part of your body, and of every other living thing, is made up of cells. In human beings, some cells divide to create new cells every twelve to twenty-four hours (unlike bacterial

Breast Anatomy

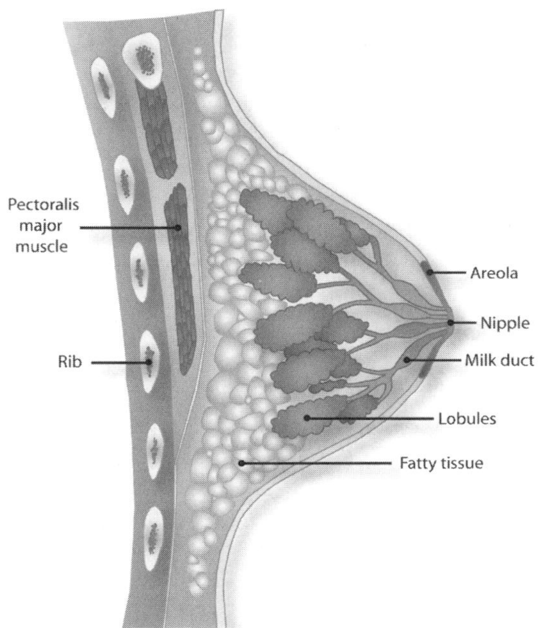

cells, for example, which can divide every twenty to thirty minutes). In the normal, orderly cell-renewal process, cells reproduce just fast enough to replace the ones that die off, thus keeping your blood and organs healthy.

When cells become abnormal and start to divide uncontrollably, the condition is called cancer. In a process called *neoplasia*, the cells mutate and start dividing helter-skelter. The new mutant cells behave in the same way as their "parents," eventually forming an abnormal growth, or *tumor*. Tumor cells not only act differently from normal cells, but they also look different under a microscope.

Some tumors are *benign*—not cancerous. Benign tumors do not spread, so surgically removing them usually solves the problem for good. By contrast, a *malignant* (cancerous) tumor—if not detected and treated early—can spread from its original site to other parts of the body in a process called *metastasis.* Malignant tumors are usually removed by surgery and treated with one or more additional types of therapy, depending on how large they are and whether they have metastasized.

Where and How Cancer Forms in the Breast

Most breast cancers develop in the lobes or ducts of the breast. Scientists, though still learning exactly how this occurs, have identified certain risk factors—some proven, others more questionable at this point. It is helpful to be aware of all of them.

Risk Factors for Breast Cancer

Hereditary and Genetic Risks

Most of the time—in about 70 percent of breast cancer cases—there is no known history of the disease in the woman's family. In such cases, the disease is called *sporadic* breast cancer. In another 20 percent of cases, at least one relative—more often an aunt or a grandmother than a mother or a sister—has had breast cancer. When this family history exists, the disease may be referred to as *polygenic* breast cancer.

Even with a family history of polygenic breast cancer, many family members do not develop the illness. It increases a woman's lifetime risk only from about 3.3 percent (with no other known risk factors) to less than 8 percent—so the odds of not getting breast cancer are still greatly in her favor.

Less commonly—in 5 to 10 percent of all breast cancers—the disease is clearly passed from generation to generation, usually through genes *BRCA1* (pronounced BRACK-uh 1) and *BRCA2.* Everyone has two copies of each of these genes, whose usual job is to suppress tumors, not to cause them. So, it is not the genes themselves but the rare *mutations* (structural changes) in BRCA1 or BRCA2 that are responsible for truly *hereditary* breast cancer. But for these genes to give rise to cancer, both copies must have mutated.

A father or mother with one mutated gene, whether or not he or she develops cancer, has a fifty-fifty chance of passing the mutation to the next generation. Accordingly, a woman can have hereditary breast cancer while her mother and sisters stay cancer-free.

A woman who inherits a mutated BRCA1 gene (more common than with BRCA2, about which less is known) has a lifetime breast-cancer risk of 50 to 70 percent—quite a large variation. She also is at greater-than-average risk for ovarian cancer. Whether or not she develops cancer depends on whether the second copy of the gene mutates, which can happen as a result of other risk factors or for reasons that are not yet understood. Other genetic mutations have been associated with an increased breast cancer risk as well. Family history is very helpful in deciding what mutations to test for.

Environmental Risks

Every day, we are exposed to toxins in the form of pesticides, herbicides, cleaning solvents, chemical waste, food additives, certain plastics, and many other substances. Some are known *carcinogens* (cancer-causing agents). Others have been linked to higher rates of cancer among people exposed to them, but the cause has not been scientifically proven.

> ***I don't care how many breasts my mom has. I'm just happy she's okay.***
> ***—Gail, 13***

Hormonal Risks

Compared to the general population, a woman is at greater risk for breast cancer if she has been exposed to higher levels of estrogen over her lifetime. This exposure can be entirely natural, due to the factors listed below:

- early onset of menstrual periods (before age 12)
- late menopause (after 55)
- late first pregnancy (after 30)
- no pregnancies

Also contributing to lifetime estrogen exposure are medicines that contain estrogen, such as birth-control pills and drugs taken to ease menopausal symptoms. Most researchers doubt that the synthetic hormones in birth-control pills pose much of a breast cancer risk. Some studies suggest a slightly higher risk among long-term users of "the Pill" and among women who started using it as teenagers—but that risk drops dramatically when the pill is stopped.

Long-term estrogen-replacement therapy, during and after menopause, is another risk factor that diminishes when use of the hormone is stopped. Certain hormone combinations, however, are more carcinogenic than treatment with estrogen alone. These include estrogen and progesterone (or *progestin*, synthetic progesterone), which is sold under several labels, and estrogen and testosterone (usually sold as Estratest).

If you're taking a prescription drug for menopause symptoms, ask your doctor if it contains one of these combinations and, if so, whether you should switch to another drug.

After my diagnosis, I dealt with anxiety by saying, 'I'm alive today and will live today to the hilt.' By fearing death, I figured I was dying all the time instead of living.
—Suzanne, 58

DES (diethylstilbestrol), a synthetic estrogen, was prescribed from the 1940s until 1971 to prevent pregnancy complications. Women who took this drug have a slightly elevated breast cancer risk. Daughters who were exposed to DES in their mothers' wombs do not appear to share this risk, though it's impossible to be certain until more of these daughters reach their forties, fifties, and beyond—the ages at which breast cancer is more likely to occur.

Radiation Exposure

Women who have had radiation to the chest—perhaps as treatment for cancers such as Hodgkin's disease or for conditions such as tuberculosis or breast inflammation *(mastitis)*—are at greater risk for breast cancer. (Radiation as a treatment for nonmalignant diseases ended by the 1960s, once the risks were understood.)

If you have been treated with radiation to the chest, you should begin regular breast self-examination and annual mammograms no later than ten years after the radiation treatment began. These precautions are all the more important if you were exposed during puberty, since developing breasts are especially vulnerable.

The small amount of radiation delivered in chest X-rays and mammograms are not a cause for concern—except possibly for women who have inherited mutated BRCA1 or BRCA2 genes.

Diet and Alcohol Use

If you are overweight, especially if you put on those excess pounds during adulthood, your risk is higher than other women's. The same is true if you drink alcohol. The more you drink and the younger you start, the higher the risk. As little as three alcoholic drinks a week increases the risk.

> ***Maintaining a positive attitude is very important as you go through the treatment. It may be the best medicine there is during breast cancer treatment.***
>
> *—Jan, 69*

Nationality and Ethnicity

North America has one of the highest incidences of breast cancer in the world, followed by Western Europe, Australia/New Zealand, and Northern Europe. The incidence is lowest in China and central Africa. Genetic factors play a part, but environment and lifestyle may be equally important, since second- and third-generation immigrants to the United States are more likely to get breast cancer than their nonimmigrant relatives.

In the United States, white women are at slightly greater risk for breast cancer than African-American women, but the death rate is higher among African-Americans. The risk is lower among Native American, Hispanic, and Asian women.

Age and Gender

Clearly, a great many things carry some degree of risk for breast cancer, but the fact is, most women who develop the disease have not encountered any of them—apart from being female and getting older, neither of which you can do anything about. You can do everything in your power to stay healthy and minimize your other risk factors. And you can—since no prevention measure is foolproof against breast cancer—spare no effort to find your cancer early if it should develop.

2

Getting a Diagnosis

You may tell yourself, "it's probably nothing,"—that lump or thickness you think you feel in your breast. Perhaps you're thinking you should wait a while before going to see your doctor. Maybe you're thinking it really isn't a lump and that it will go away. Perhaps you're thinking about the fact that you're healthy and take care of yourself, so you shouldn't have breast cancer.

Still, it is important to investigate any suspicious change in your breast. And schedule that mammogram and annual physical. Breast cancer tumors that can be felt are usually discovered by you or by your doctor during a routine physical. Most lumps that can't be felt show up in mammograms.

If you find a lump, the next step is to get it *diagnosed*—to find out whether it is caused by cancer or something else. Odds are, it's something else. Only about one out of five breast lumps is cancerous.

Methods of Examining the Breasts

Breast Self-Examination (BSE)

Many women discover their own cancers during a *breast self-examination* (*BSE*). That's why every woman should examine her breasts every month. BSE should become routine as soon as the breasts develop, or by age 20 at the latest.

Because the breasts tend to swell during the menstrual period, premenopausal women should perform BSE three to five days after their period ends. Postmenopausal women should examine their breasts on the same day every month, so that the date itself is a reminder.

Some women, especially those in high-risk categories, avoid BSE because they are afraid of what they might find. This avoidance is understandable. It's also unhealthy, emotionally and physically. Frequent, habitual self-examination is by far the best way to discover a cancer while it is small and highly treatable, and finding a small tumor is much better than finding a large one.

One excuse some women use for not doing BSE is that their breasts are always lumpy—the result of normal, benign masses called *cysts* or *fibrocystic changes*. This condition is often mistakenly referred to as "fibrocystic disease," but it is not an illness.

My diagnosis was unbelievable to me. The radiologist kept saying she was concerned about my mammogram and I kept saying it was just scar tissue from a previous biopsy. Then it dawned on me that she was trying to tell me she thought I had breast cancer.
—Kristine, 51

If you chronically have benign masses in your breasts, you might assume that you wouldn't notice a new lump or one that is unusual. But if you examine your breasts regularly, you'll learn the "terrain." Once you're familiar with the texture and the pattern of cysts in your breasts, you *will* detect changes, even small ones.

Every month, use both BSE techniques: one lying down and one standing before a mirror. Lying down, you'll examine your breasts with your hands. In front of a mirror, you'll inspect them with your eyes. Some warning signs are more apparent by feel and others by sight. Here's what you should be on the alert for:

- a lump or thickening in the breast, surrounding area, or armpit
- swelling, redness, or rash
- puckering or dimpling of the skin

- skin texture like that of an orange (a condition called peau d'orange)
- itchiness, soreness, or scaling of the nipple
- drawing-in (retraction) of the nipple or another part of the breast
- unusual warmth that feels feverish in or near the breast
- any change in breast size, shape, or symmetry
- unusual pain in a part of the breast, armpit, or surrounding area
- bloody discharge from the nipple

To examine your breasts while lying down:

1. Place a small pillow under your right shoulder; then raise your right arm, and rest the back of your hand on your forehead. This position flattens the breast and makes it easier to examine.
2. Using the pads of the three middle fingers of your left hand, make small circular motions to examine your breast with light, medium, and then firm pressure. Don't lift your fingers but keep them flat as you do this.
3. Use an up-and-down pattern, as if following narrow vertical stripes, to cover the entire breast and surrounding area–from collarbone to lower bra line to breastbone, and including the armpit.
4. Repeat steps 1 through 3 using the right hand to examine the left breast.

You can examine your breasts this way in the shower or bathtub, although if you're not lying down you lose the advantage of your breasts being flattened, which makes abnormalities easier to find. On the other hand, slick, soapy skin makes small changes more noticeable. You can get the soapy-skin effect while lying down by applying a smooth lotion or placing a piece of slippery fabric (such as satin) over your breast while you examine it.

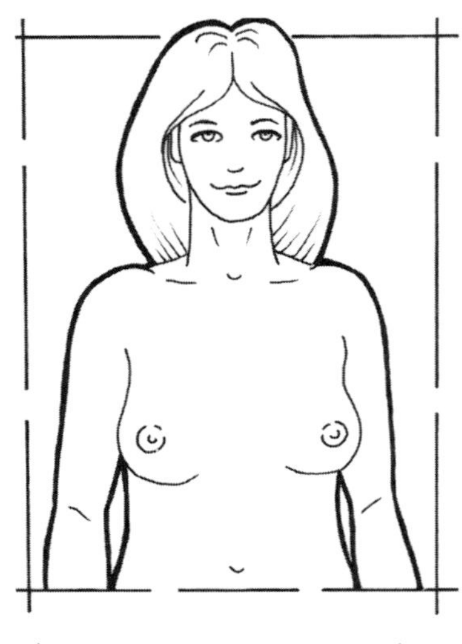

Arms at side.

Compare symmetry.

Look for changes in:

- shape
- color

Check for:

- puckering
- dimpling
- skin changes
- nipple discharge

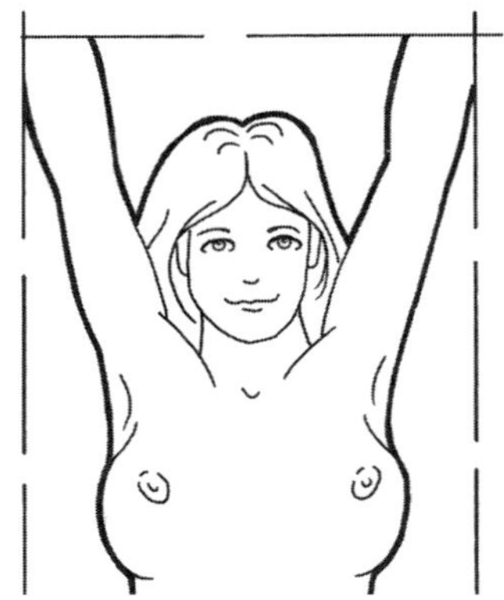

Arms over head.

Check front and side view for:

- symmetry
- puckering
- dimpling

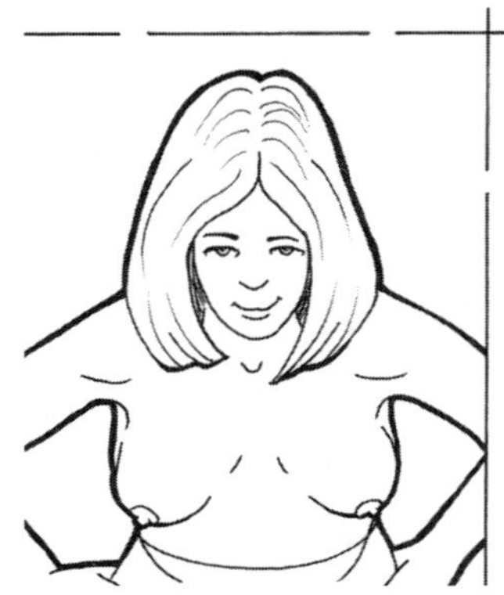

Hands on hips, press down, and bend forward.

Check for:

- symmetry
- nipple direction
- general appearance

Lie down.

- Place a pillow under right shoulder.
- Raise right arm above head.
- Use the pads of the three middle fingers of your left hand.

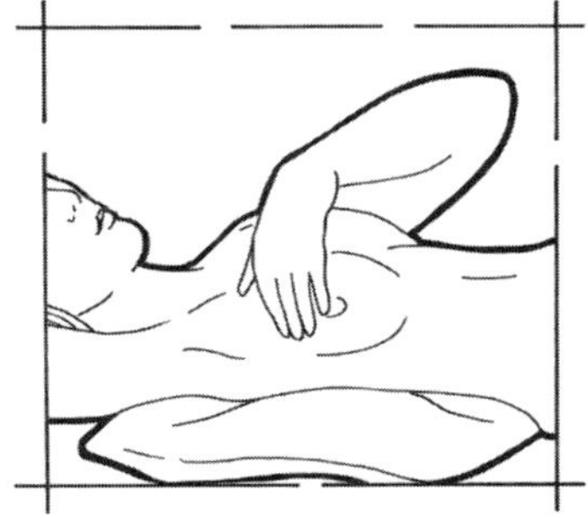

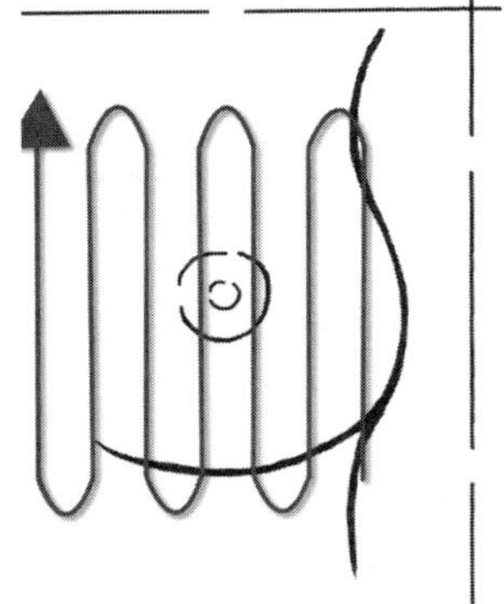

Examine area vertically from:

- across breastbone
- up to collarbone
- back to armpit

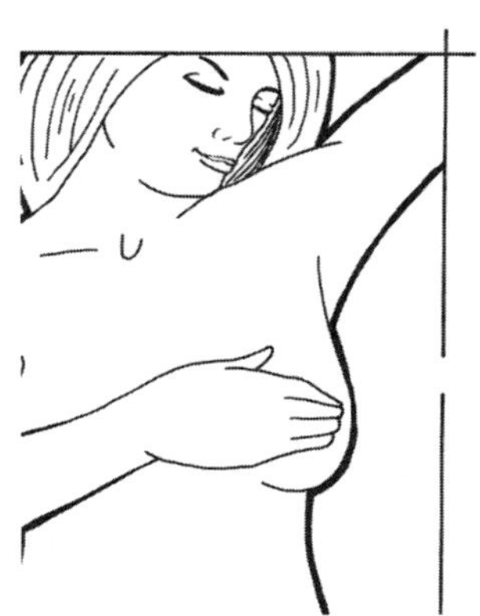

Examine entire area.

- Use vertical stripe pattern.
- Use light, medium, and firm pressure.
- Move fingers in dime-size circles.

To examine your breasts in the mirror, look for any of the warning signs listed above. Do this in each of the following positions:

- with your arms down at your sides
- with both arms held straight up
- with your hands pressed against your hips to tighten the chest muscles and bending forward at the waist

If you notice a warning sign during BSE, or at any other time, see your doctor. Don't put it off, and if the doctor's office staff tries to schedule your visit for "the next available appointment" six months from now, ask to speak with the doctor's nurse or with the doctor.

Do not assume that a lump can't be cancer if it moves (or doesn't move) or if it is hard (or soft), tender (or painless), or regular (or irregular) in shape. *Any* new lump or thickening should be examined by a doctor, regardless of its characteristics. If you are worried about a lump, insist on imaging studies (such as ultrasound or MRI) or a biopsy. You deserve a clear answer, and no doctor can provide one just by feeling the lump.

Waiting for test results, for information, is the hardest. When you're afraid, any wait at all seems too long.
—Ann, 53

It is never safe to stop doing BSE. It should be a lifelong habit, even if you have had a mastectomy or lumpectomy. After surgery, begin examining the incision right away for changes, bumps, rigid areas, or discoloration, and search for lumps above and below the collarbone and in the armpit. Practicing BSE on the opposite breast is extremely important, too. Survivors of some types of breast cancer are at high risk for a new breast cancer in the opposite breast.

Clinical Examination

Though a clinical examination is not a substitute for BSE, you should always have a clinical breast exam as part of your yearly checkup. Your doctor will feel the breasts and breast area for thickening or lumps, check for visible warning signs, and ask about breast tenderness or changes you might have experienced, your breast care, your medical history, and your family's medical history.

An experienced medical professional is usually more skilled than the patient at feeling the difference between a benign lump and a malignant one, but, as mentioned above, he or she can't be certain whether a lump or another symptom indicates cancer. If the clinical exam raises suspicions of cancer, further diagnostic tests will be needed. The most common ones are described below.

Mammography

A *mammogram* is an X-ray of the breast—simple, widely available, and lifesaving. Scientists trying to understand why the number of breast cancer deaths fell 24 percent between 1990 and 2000 found that mammograms were the most important factor, followed by new ways of treating the disease.

> ***When I was diagnosed, tears came to my eyes, but I was more worried about my husband and two boys. How would they handle it if something happened to me? My main thought was helping them get through this.***
> ***—Julianne, 54***

Having a mammogram takes only a few minutes. It's simply a matter of standing next to a mammography machine while a technician positions your breast on a small, square plate, compresses it against another plate, tells you to hold your breath, and "snaps" the image. It's over in seconds. The process is repeated—two images for each breast—and all you feel is a brief pinch during the short time your breast is squeezed between the plates.

The images are captured either on film, like a photographic negative, or on solid-state detectors similar to those in digital cameras. In the latter case, the image is called a digital mammogram. Digital mammography exposes the breast to even less radiation than a film mammogram, produces more detailed images, and more accurately depicts the comparatively dense breasts of younger women. Whichever type of mammogram you have, a radiologist will interpret the images and you'll learn the results in a few days. Ideally, the same radiologist will read all your mammograms and compare your most recent images with your older ones.

Mammograms—whether on film or digital—are done for either screening or diagnostic purposes. A screening mammogram searches for early cancers that cannot be felt, while a diagnostic mammogram inspects a breast lump that can be felt or an abnormality detected in a screening mammogram. Thus, if you or your doctor finds a lump in your breast, a diagnostic mammogram is usually the next step.

If your breasts are healthy as far as you know, ask your doctor when to start having regular screening mammograms and how often you should have them. If you're in a high-risk category, she might want you to have your first mammogram while you're still in your twenties.

Digital mammography is the standard of care, and it is recommended that you seek out a breast center or clinic that offers digital mammography.

The following is a common schedule for mammography:

- A baseline mammogram, as a reference point to which future mammograms can be compared, when you are between 35 and 40.
- An annual mammogram after age 40.
- An annual mammogram if you have ever had breast cancer.
- If your mother or sister has had breast cancer, an annual mammogram starting when you are ten years younger than the earliest-diagnosed relative. For example, if your mother developed breast cancer at 45 and your sister at 32, you should start having annual mammograms at 22.

Don't be alarmed if your mammogram shows abnormalities and your doctor wants to do additional tests. Only 5 to 10 percent of "suspicious" abnormalities turn out to be breast cancer. False-positive results are so common that most women who

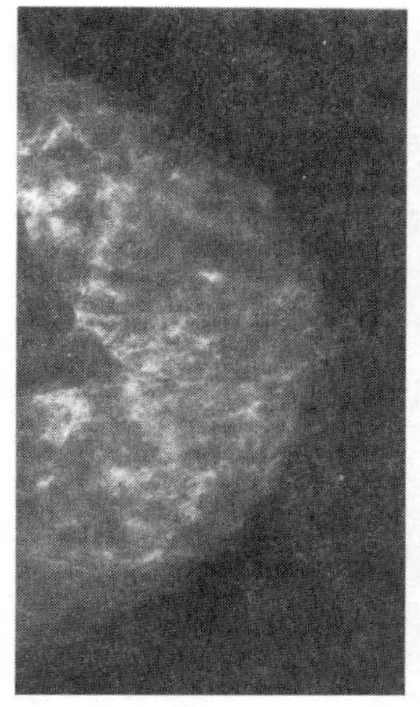

A normal mammogram.

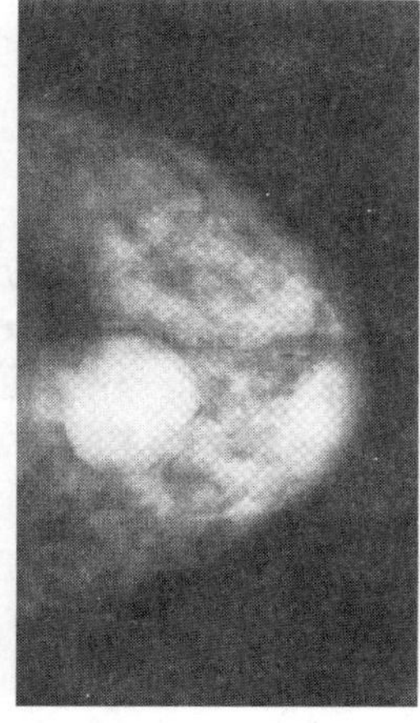

Mammogram showing cysts with smooth edges.

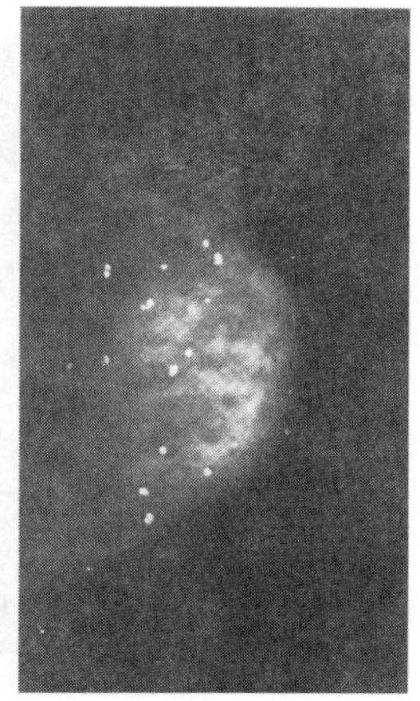

Mammogram with benign calcifications scattered throughout.

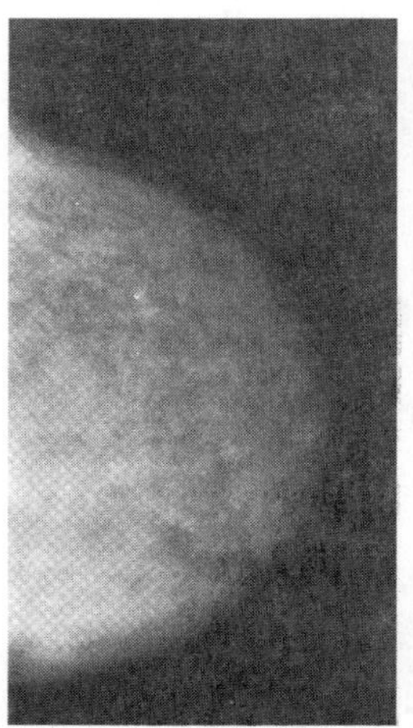

Mammogram showing a dense pattern, usually seen in younger women.

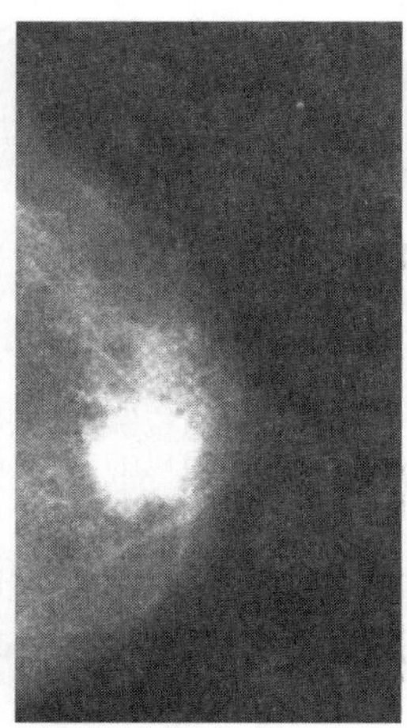

Mammogram showing cancerous growth. Note the irregular edges.

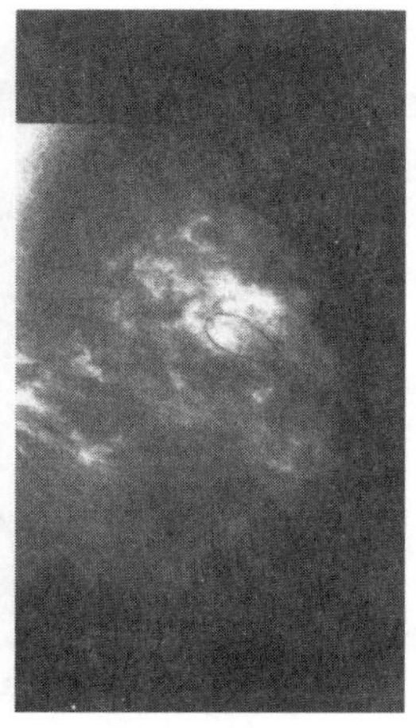

Mammogram with cluster micro-calcifications. These clusters are usually benign, but may be cancerous.

have regular mammograms will eventually get that dreaded phone call or letter asking them to return for further tests, only to find that there is nothing wrong.

Be grateful for false-positives, and for your doctor's diligence in following up on a suspicious abnormality that turns out to be harmless. The inconvenience and expense of follow-up diagnostic studies (usually another mammogram or an ultrasound) are easily outweighed by the many lives mammography saves, and by your peace of mind.

False-negative results are also possible, particularly in women with dense breasts. Mammography simply fails to "see" 10 to 20 percent of cancers in these dense tissues. Ask your doctor or your mammogram technician if you have dense breast tissue. If the answer is yes, your doctor may agree to order additional tests, such as ultrasonography.

Abnormal mammogram findings that must be investigated include:

- a white, starburst-shaped (spiculated) mass or nodule (as distinct from the clear, smooth edges of harmless cysts and benign tumors)
- uneven density (Dense areas in the breast are thicker than normal and whiter than the surrounding tissue. If these densities are larger in one breast, or appear in a different part of one breast than in the other, they may be cause for concern.)
- microcalcifications (calcium particles)—very common and usually benign, but if clustered in a certain way, might indicate cancer
- any change since your previous mammogram

Ultrasonography

We have seen that mammography is a highly useful diagnostic test but is not foolproof. When both mammography and *ultrasonography* are used, a clearer picture can emerge.

Ultrasonography bounces sound waves off tissues and organs. The sound waves bounce back as patterns of echoes, which can be converted to images and projected onto a computer monitor. The procedure is painless, and you won't hear or see either the sound waves or the echoes.

To gather these images, an ultrasonography technician spreads a gel on your breast so that the sound waves can pass through more easily. Then he or she will pass a microphone-like device, called a *transducer,* over your skin. The transducer both emits the sound waves and transmits the echoes to the computer.

According to some researchers, mammography plus ultrasonography can find about 17 percent more tumors than mammography alone. Sometimes, ultrasonography can detect whether a lump in the breast is filled with fluid and most likely is a cyst, or if it is solid tissue that might or might not be cancer.

Magnetic Resonance Imaging (MRI)

Magnetic resonance imaging (MRI) uses powerful magnets and radio waves to produce computer images of selected body tissues. Among other things, these images reveal the blood vessels in different types of tissue. Cancer spreads by forming new blood vessels, so cancer tissues are often highly *vascular,* containing a great many more blood vessels than normal tissues.

Hundreds of images are taken, each representing a thin slice of tissue. A computer combines the images, which are read and interpreted by a radiologist.

If you are having MRI to detect breast cancer, you will probably be injected with a dye that is absorbed more quickly by cancerous tissue—where more blood vessels cluster—than by normal tissue or benign tumors. The radiologist will look for concentrations of this dye that might suggest a malignancy.

MRI can be an extremely useful and accurate diagnostic tool. False-positive and false-negative results are possible, of course, as with any test. For example, some nonmalignant tumors are highly vascular and thus appear malignant on MRI. Likewise, slow-growing cancers with relatively few blood vessels may look like normal tissue and yield false-negative results.

MRI is painless but can be time-consuming (thirty minutes to two hours), tedious, and noisy. You'll have to lie still most of the time as your bed moves slowly through a large cylinder. Ask your doctor how long the MRI will take and whether you can listen to music or an audiobook through the headphones provided. If you're claustrophobic, your doctor will probably prescribe something to relax you without putting you to sleep.

Because MRI is expensive and is unavailable in many areas, it is not as commonly used as mammography or ultrasonography for detecting breast cancer. Insurance may cover MRI for lumpectomy candidates (in order to confirm that the cancer is confined to the tumor) and in cases where a strong family history of breast cancer exists or a mutated BRCA1 or BRCA2 gene is present.

Breast Cancer in Men

Although it is rare, breast cancer does occur in men. Approximately 2,000 men are diagnosed annually. Symptoms include lump in the breast, nipple pain, inverted nipple, nipple discharge, sores on the nipple, and enlarged lymph nodes under the arm. Treatment for men is similar to that for women.

Diagnosing with Biopsy

If other tests haven't ruled out cancer, you and your doctor will schedule a biopsy—an outpatient procedure in which cells, sample tissue, or an entire tumor is removed from the body for microscopic examination. Then, a *pathologist*—a doctor who diagnoses disease from tissue or blood samples—examines the sample under a microscope, and may perform other tests on it as well, to see if cancer cells are present.

It's important for the surgeon who performs your biopsy to remove ample tissue from the sites where cancer is suspected. A biopsy, properly performed, can give a precise diagnosis and is the only sure way to establish whether a lump is malignant. For a tumor to be pronounced benign, the clinical exam, the mammogram, and the biopsy must all agree on the finding. For a cancer diagnosis, the biopsy alone is conclusive.

You should insist on a biopsy for any persistent or questionable lump, regardless of your family medical history or level of risk. It is your right to do so, even if others try to convince you that a clinical examination is sufficient.

There are several types of biopsies. The one your doctor recommends may depend on the size and exact location of the lump, the number of suspicious areas in the breast, and your own preference. Asking questions ahead of time, such as the ones suggested below, may lessen any anxiety you may feel about your biopsy.

- Which type of biopsy should I have?
- Will I be awake during the biopsy?
- How much tissue will be removed?
- What tests will be performed on the tissue sample?
- What are the risks and possible side effects of my biopsy?
- When and where will I learn the results and who will report them to me?

Types of Biopsies

The three major types of biopsies are *fine-needle aspira-*

When to Have MRI Screening for Breast Cancer

An MRI is recommended in addition to a mammogram if you:

- have a strong family history of breast or ovarian cancer
- have been determined to have a lifetime risk of breast cancer
- have dense breast tissue and a previous breast cancer was not detected by mammogram
- have had radiation to the chest between the ages of 10 and 30
- or a close relative has had any of these syndromes:
  - *Cowden Syndrome*—a rare disorder, causing noncancerous tumors on the skin or in the lining of the mouth and nose
  - *Li-Fraumeni Syndrome (LFS)*—a hereditary predisposition to cancer
  - *Bannayan-Riley-Ruvalcaba Syndrome (BRR)*—an uncommon condition, causing noncancerous polyps of the small and large intestines

MRI guidelines are from the American Cancer Society.

tion, core (large-needle) biopsy, and *surgical biopsy.* Most biopsies are performed using a local anesthetic, which numbs the area from which the sample will be taken. Occasionally, more extensive biopsies are done with the patient under anesthesia.

Fine-needle aspiration (FNA) is the least invasive type of biopsy. It is used when lumps can be easily felt and located. The FNA procedure removes a small sample of cells through a narrow, hypodermic-type needle. Your doctor will insert the biopsy needle into the lump or thickening, then draw fluid into the syringe. A *cytologist* (a specialized pathologist who examines cells, rather than tissue or blood, for the presence of disease) then examines this fluid in the laboratory. If no cancer cells are found, your doctor may double-check the results with a more extensive biopsy, withdrawing a larger sample from the lump.

Large-needle or core biopsy takes a small, cylindrical sample of tissue from the lump rather than withdrawing only fluid. If the lump can be felt, the biopsy needle is inserted directly into it, without computer guidance. If the doctor can't feel the lump, he or she will use computer imaging or ultrasonography to guide the needle to the lump. This type of procedure is referred to as *image-guided* or *stereotactic core biopsy.*

Other types of biopsies include the *Mammotome (*or *vacuum-assisted)* biopsy, which is a core biopsy that uses a larger tube, with the help of suction, to withdraw more breast tissue than in a traditional core biopsy. An *advanced breast biopsy instrumentation (ABBI)* also withdraws a larger sample, using a rotating circular knife to excise the tissue. Some feel it is preferable to get a needle biopsy rather than an open surgical biopsy, since a needle biopsy does not disrupt the field for a later sentinel node biopsy, should one be necessary. As you may recall, the sentinel node is the first node that lymph fluid reaches after passing through the breast.

A negative core biopsy—one that shows no evidence of cancer—may or may not be conclusive. If there is a strong suspicion of cancer, based on an earlier imaging procedure or clinical exam, your doctor might schedule a surgical biopsy. But if a newly detected tumor "feels benign," and looks benign in imag-

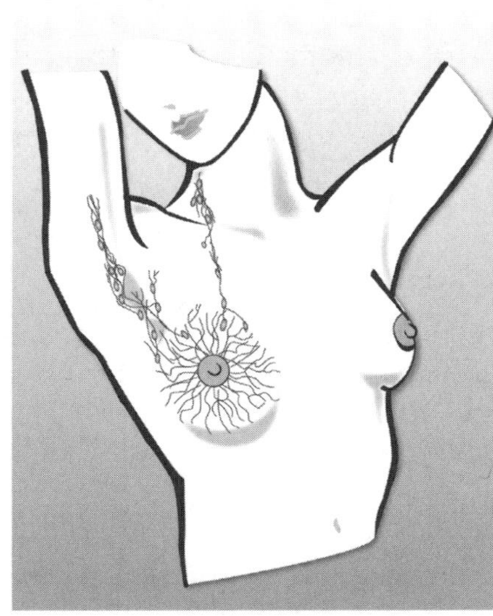

The lymph nodes are small, bean-shaped glands. The illustration above shows the location of lymph nodes in the area of the breast, underarm, and neck.

ing tests, then a negative core biopsy will be seen as confirming this assumption, and surgical biopsy will be unnecessary.

Surgical or open biopsy removes, through an incision, all or part of a lump or suspicious area for examination by a pathologist. *Incisional biopsy* involves removal of a tissue sample large enough for the pathologist to make a confident diagnosis, and the results of this procedure are usually conclusive. *Excisional biopsy* is, in essence, a lumpectomy—the entire lump and a small amount of the healthy tissue surrounding it are removed. Your doctor may choose excisional biopsy for small tumors that show no indications of spreading. If cancer is present, it will thus be removed in this single procedure.

Test Results and Tumor Characteristics

Waiting anxiously for the results can be the worst part of a biopsy, so ask your doctor when and how you'll learn your diagnosis. At the time of your biopsy, you might want to schedule a post-biopsy appointment with your doctor to discuss the results. It's up to you. If you do have breast cancer, would you prefer to get the news in person, with your partner there to support you? The alternative might be to wait for a phone call that could come at any time and under undesirable circumstances.

If the biopsy is positive, the combined results of all your diagnostic tests will show the characteristics of the cancer and will help your physician decide on the best course of treatment.

Size of the Tumor

Small tumors measure up to 2 centimeters (less than an inch) in diameter. Medium-size tumors are between 2 and 5 centimeters (up to 2 inches), and large tumors are more than 5 centimeters (2 inches).

Presence of Cancer Cells in Blood Vessels or Lymph Vessels

Because blood and lymph fluid circulate throughout the body, they can carry cancer cells almost anywhere. Thus, cancer cells in the blood vessels or lymph vessels signify a greater likelihood of metastasis to other parts of the body.

Appearance of the Cancer Cells

As normal cells mature, they take on distinctive, specialized shapes, depending on their function. Mature breast cells look very different from, say, mature skin cells or liver cells.

Well-differentiated breast cancer cells are typical of slow-growing cancers. They look much like normal, mature breast cells, with clearly defined boundaries. Very different in appearance are *poorly differentiated* breast cancer cells which have indistinct boundaries. These immature cells are found in aggressive tumors, in which the cells divide so quickly that they don't have time to mature.

Aneuploid cancer cells indicate a more aggressive disease than do *diploid* cancer cells. *Diploid* human cells have the normal forty-six chromosomes—two sets of twenty-three, one from each of your parents. *Chromosomes* are made up of protein and DNA, the genetic material that determines whether you have "your father's eyes" or "your mother's freckles." Aneuploid cells have more or fewer than forty-six chromosomes, so they also have abnormal amounts of DNA.

Rate of Cancer Cell Reproduction

A measurement called the *S-phase fraction* establishes, on a scale of 1 to 100, the percentage of cells that are dividing in the tumor. Higher numbers—greater than 7 percent—may indicate faster-growing and therefore more aggressive cancers.

Hormone Dependency

The female hormones *estrogen* and *progesterone* are largely responsible for a woman's reproductive functions, including *lactation* (milk production in the breast). These hormones circulate throughout the body but interact only with cells that have special *receptors* where the hormones can attach themselves.

These hormones interact with cells in more than one way. Estrogen, for example, sometimes stimulates cell growth and sometimes blocks it. In the case of cancer, it is important to know which role estrogen plays. This can be determined by examining cancer cells to see which kind of hormone receptor, if any, is present. Testing cancer cells for estrogen and progesterone receptors can help doctors understand how aggressive the cancer might be and what kinds of therapy would be most effective.

I felt so afraid after my diagnosis, even ashamed, because breasts are so personal. My first reaction was to hide and not let anyone know. But it helped so much to talk to someone. Talk to other women who have been through it.

—Billie, 48

Genetic Factors

Every invasive breast cancer should be tested for the HER2/neu (also called c-erB-2) receptor. HER2, short for "human epidermal growth factor receptor 2," is a gene—one of the thousands of genes that make up chromosomes and control the structure and activity of every cell in your body. They do this by producing, or "expressing," specific proteins to do specific jobs. The HER2 gene expresses the HER2/neu protein.

In 20 to 30 percent of breast cancers, the cells have more than two copies of this gene and express too much HER2/neu. The more copies of the gene there are, the more the protein is overexpressed and the more quickly the cancer is likely to grow.

Your doctor may also test the tumor for mutation of the *p53 gene* and schedule a *Ki-67* test. The p53 gene is normally a tumor suppressor that helps regulate cell growth; thus, an abnormal p53 gene can indicate uncontrolled cell growth. Ki-67 is a protein whose growth rate in cancer cells can be measured to reveal how fast a tumor is growing.

A K-67 test is now evaluated in pre-and post-therapy (chemotherapy or radiation) to determine early whether treatment is effective or needs to be changed.

You may find yourself exhausted by what seems like a never-ending barrage of tests. Understanding why your doctor orders a particular test and what information it provides may help you keep it all in perspective.

Testing for Risk of Recurrence

Whether or not a cancer spreads depends partially on the behavior of genes within the tumor. Thanks to technology, newer tests are now available to examine the genes of breast cancer tissue. These tests serve as indicators of whether a woman's risk of recurrence is low or high. Accordingly, the test results help doctors and patients choose the best line of postsurgical treatment. For example, if the risk is low, doctors may recommend hormone therapy. If the risk is high, doctors may recommend a more aggressive treatment that includes chemotherapy.

I highly recommend going to a breast cancer support group. You learn the tricks of the trade, hints for coping. No one really understands unless they've been through it.
—Mary, 43

One such genetic test, *Mammaprint*, is used to evaluate tumor tissue. This test assesses seventy-one genes and determines the likelihood of cancer recurring within five to ten years of the initial diagnosis. Mammaprint can be used to test women under age 60 who have Stage I or Stage II breast cancer with negatives nodes and tumors no larger than five centimeters.

Another test, *Oncotype DX*, provides information for post-menopausal women with early–stage (Stage I or II), lymph node negative, estrogen receptor-positive breast cancer. The test assesses twenty-one genes and indicates whether a woman is at low or high risk for recurrence.

Types of Breast Cancer

Ductal Cancer

The most common form of breast cancer, ductal cancer starts in the cells that line the milk ducts. Between 70 and 80 percent of breast cancers begin in the linings of these tube-like tissues, whose purpose is to transport milk from the milk-producing lobes to the nipple during breastfeeding.

When abnormal cells are present but have not spread through the walls of the milk ducts, the condition is called *ductal carcinoma in situ,* or DCIS. *In situ* means "in the original place." DCIS is considered *preinvasive* because the abnormal cells are malignant and capable of becoming *invasive,* spreading into surrounding breast structures and beyond. For this reason, the first treatment for DCIS is surgery, either lumpectomy or total mastectomy.

> ***Cancer brings so many issues to the table—sexual, financial, school, parenting, work. A couple who works together through these issues, which normally would be experienced over a longer period of time, will be brought closer together.***
> ***—Holly, oncology social worker***

Invasive ductal cancer usually is found in a single site, not at several locations throughout the breast or in the opposite breast. The overall risk of *bilateral* ductal cancer (that is, ductal cancer in both breasts) is only 0.8 percent per year after the initial diagnosis.

A DCIS lesion occasionally feels like a lump or a thickening of the duct, but it is more commonly detected first on a screening mammogram, where it can show up as a small cluster of calcium deposits called *microcalcifications.* Unfortunately, only about 50 percent of DCIS cases develop microcalcifications that can be seen on a mammogram. If cancer is suspected but is not visible on a mammogram, your doctor may use ductal lavage to flush out cells from the milk-duct lining. These cells are then analyzed for cancer. Otherwise, a DCIS lesion may be discovered incidentally, when a biopsy is performed on a breast lump, or go undetected until it becomes invasive.

Lobular Cancer

About 10 percent of breast cancers are *lobular carcinomas.* Lobular cancer begins in the milk-producing lobules and may become invasive, spreading into surrounding breast tissue.

Lobular carcinoma is less common than ductal cancer, but has the potential to affect both breasts more than other types of breast cancer. In about 30 percent of cases, this cancer is found in both breasts; it typically feels like a thickening in the breast in the area from the nipple to the underarm. Sometimes, the skin will pucker. Lobular carcinoma does *not* usually show up on a mammogram. An MRI scan is recommended in cases of lobular cancer to make sure all the sites are detected.

Lobular carcinoma in situ (LCIS) refers to the presence of abnormal cells in the lobes. LCIS cells are not malignant, and the cells themselves do not develop into invasive cancer; however, these abnormal cells are signals of a risk that either lobular or ductal cancer will develop in either breast or both.

> ***When I walk into a breast cancer patient's hospital room and tell her I am a 10-year survivor, I can see how good that makes her feel. I remember when I was lying in my hospital bed, I didn't think anyone survived.***
> ***—Dianna, 44***

LCIS is rarely visible on a mammogram and is usually found during a biopsy on a breast lump. Treatment is either bilateral mastectomy or close observation. In some cases, LCIS is treated with the drug *tamoxifen*, which has been shown to prevent breast cancer in many high-risk women.

Other Breast Cancers

There are several less common types of breast cancers, each accounting for only about 1 to 1.5 percent of all breast cancers. The prognosis varies among these rare cancers.

Inflammatory breast cancer is an aggressive form of the disease that is often overlooked or misdiagnosed as infection. There is usually no lump to draw attention to inflammatory breast cancer. Rather, the cancer tends to be *diffuse,* or scattered—beginning in the ducts, spreading rapidly through the lymph vessels beneath the skin, eventually blocking the flow of lymph, and sometimes spreading along the chest wall. When symptoms appear, the breast may swell, feel warm or unusually painful, and take on a reddish tinge. The skin texture may change, developing ridges or thickening. When the skin looks pitted like the outside of an orange, the condition is known as *peau d' orange.* "Peau" is French for skin.

Other warning signs of inflammatory breast cancer include:

- a mark like a bruise that does not go away
- nipple retraction
- bloody discharge from the nipple
- itching that isn't relieved by creams or ointments
- swelling in lymph nodes under the arm or above the collarbone

Warmth or pain in the breast, redness, and swelling are symptoms of breast infection, or *mastitis,* for which antibiotics are typically prescribed. When antibiotics don't clear up the problem, the next step is usually a biopsy.

Inflammatory breast cancer is a highly aggressive and dangerous form of the disease. Thus, it requires aggressive and immediate treatment, often in the form of chemotherapy followed by surgery, radiation therapy, additional chemotherapy, and hormonal therapy. If you have any inflammatory breast cancer symptoms, by all means see your doctor immediately and insist on a biopsy without delay.

Stages of Breast Cancer

Once your doctor knows exactly where the cancer is, additional tests will determine its *stage*—in other words, whether it has been caught early, late, or somewhere in between. Three

Staging System for Breast Cancer

Primary Tumor (T)

TX: tumor isn't found or can't be measured

T0: no evidence of primary tumor

Tis: cancer "in situ" (has not grown into the breast tissue)

T1-T4: tumor size and/or extent it has grown into the breast tissue

Regional Lymph Nodes (N)

NX: nearby lymph nodes not found or can't be measured

N0: no evidence of cancer in nearby lymph nodes

N1-N3: size, location, and/or the number of lymph nodes involved

Distant Metastases (M)

MX: metastases not found or can't be measured

M0: no evidence of distant metastases

M1: evidence of distant metastases

characteristics determine the stage of a cancer: its size, its aggressiveness, and its location in sites other than the original tumor. The likelihood of disease-free survival (the patient's *prognosis)* can depend on the stage at which the cancer is diagnosed.

In 2003, the American Joint Committee on Cancer (AJCC) revised its breast cancer-staging guidelines. One reason for the change was the introduction of sophisticated tools such as *sentinel node biopsy*, whose ability to detect even small numbers of cancer cells made it possible to stage breast cancer more accurately. As a result, sentinel node biopsy has become the standard staging procedure for breast cancer, though it is by no means the only one.

Doctors use a variety of tests for cancer staging—a blood test for liver metastases, for example; a chest X-ray for metastases to the lung; or a PET/CT scan to gather additional information about the disease at the cellular level. At the time of cancer surgery, the doctor may withdraw bone-marrow cells to be examined for evidence of *micrometastases*, free-floating cancer cells that have not yet formed a mass. (Diagnostic tests are described further in chapter 4.)

Staging Guidelines

The AJCC staging guidelines identify tumors in three ways:

- size of the original tumor (T)
- lymph node involvement (N)
- metastasis (M)

A pathologist combines the characteristics of these three elements above, tumor size, lymph node involvement, and metastasis, to assign an overall stage for the cancer. The range of these stages is 0, I, II, III, IIIA, IIIB, IIIC, or IV.

The AJCC's 2003 revisions in breast cancer staging guidelines allow more precision in staging—stage IIIC, for example, didn't exist under the old guidelines. One effect of the new guidelines has been *stage migration*: A cancer formerly identified as Stage II, for example, might become a Stage III cancer under the newer guidelines, though the cancer itself would not have changed. Many studies are under way as scientists try to learn whether the newer staging guidelines are indeed more accurate, whether they help doctors develop more effective treatment plans, and ultimately, whether they save lives.

The chart on page 32 is a general characterization of breast cancer at each stage. In the stage IIa and IIb descriptions, the phrase "microscopic disease in internal mammary nodes" refers to cancer found through sentinel node biopsy.

Stage	T	N	M	Description
Stage 0:	in situ	0	0	DCIS or LCIS
Stage I:	1	0	0	Tumor 2 cm or smaller; no spread or metastases
Stage IIa:	0-1 2	1 0	0 0	No tumor, or tumor 2 cm or smaller, with cancer in 1 to 3 axillary lymph nodes or microscopic disease in internal mammary nodes; no metastases; or Tumor 2 to 5 cm; no spread or metastases
Stage IIb:	2 3	1 0	0 0	Tumor 2 to 5 cm with cancer in 1 to 3 axillary nodes or microscopic disease in internal mammary nodes; no metastases; or Tumor larger than 5 cm; no spread or metastases
Stage IIIa:	0-2 3	2 1-2	0 0	Tumor smaller than 5 cm with cancer in 4 to 9 axillary nodes or in internal mammary nodes; no metastases; or Tumor larger than 5 cm with cancer in 1 to 9 axillary nodes or internal mammary nodes; no metastases
Stage IIIb:	4	0-2	0	Tumor has grown into chest wall or skin; cancer in 0 to 9 axillary nodes; no metastases
Stage IIIc	0-4	3	0	Tumor of any size, cancer in 10 or more axillary nodes or to other nodes on the same side; no metastases
Stage IV:	0-4	0-3	1	Tumor of any size has metastasized to distant site

3

Coping Emotionally

If you're like most women, when you heard the words "breast cancer," you may have thought you were going to die. Perhaps you have memories from years ago about family members or friends who did die from the disease. But, thanks to medical advances, this much-feared disease is no longer equated with imminent death. Although it is a life-threatening disease, breast cancer has become a treatable form of cancer, and women who develop it are living long lives.

Meanwhile, it's normal to feel a barrage of emotions upon receiving a diagnosis. Shock, fear for yourself, fear for your family, denial, and panic are all common reactions. Suddenly, you have to gather and absorb a great deal of information you never dreamed you'd need.

Sometimes you may feel overwhelmed. But you will learn to manage these new demands and to honor your feelings. You will develop strategies for coping. Soon your own, unique style of coping will become part of the wisdom breast cancer patients are eager to share; sooner than you think, you'll be helping others down the road you're traveling today.

Finding Support

Studies indicate that the diagnostic phase is an extremely stressful time for women with breast cancer. Experts say talking with others about an illness helps to relieve some of the stress. Some women turn to their significant others, relatives, or close friends. However, there are a number of other ways you can find support that will help you through this worrisome time in your life.

Meet with Your Doctor

Your regular doctor—the one you see for routine health care—may be an excellent initial source of information. Make an appointment to see him or her as soon as possible after your diagnosis. Here are some tips for your first appointment:

- Write down all your questions. Give a copy to the doctor and keep one for yourself. That way, you won't be tempted to skip some of the questions if you feel you're taking up too much of the doctor's time.
- Do some research on your own if it eases your mind. The more you know beforehand, the more new information you can absorb during your conversation.
- Don't expect to be on top of things right away. There's a lot to learn.
- Invite your mate or a close friend to go with you. Your mate can take notes and help you remember the discussion in detail.

Conduct Your Own Research

Not all your questions about breast cancer will be answered during the first meeting with your doctor. New questions will come up. Jot them down as they occur to you. Books, articles, and Web sites offer vast amounts of information, from the general to the specific.

Familiarize yourself with the library, local bookstores, and the Internet. You'll find dozens of books on breast cancer, ranging from the very technical and scientific to simple presentations of pertinent facts. Decide how much you want to know and then look for publications that will meet your needs.

If you have access to the Internet, you'll find thousands of sites that publish material online, offer books and pamphlets for sale, or both. You'll also find breast cancer organizations, chat rooms, support groups, and inspiring stories of other women who have, or have had, breast cancer. These can be enormously comforting and helpful to you at every phase of dealing with the disease. If you don't have a computer or you're unfamiliar with the Internet, most libraries have public computers and staff who can show you how to use them.

Be careful about the Web sites you visit. Not all are accurate and up-to-date. Make sure the site sponsor is reputable. If you come across confusing or conflicting information, ask your doctor about it.

Questions to Ask Your Physician

- What kind of breast cancer do I have?
- Will I lose my breast?
- What are my chances for long-term survival?
- Are further tests needed to find out whether the cancer has spread?
- How will I know which course of treatment is best for me?
- When will I begin treatment?
- How long will it take to recover from surgery and other treatments?
- Can you suggest support groups or services that might help me and my family?

Meet with a Survivor

Breast cancer survivors say that one of the most important things you can do for yourself is meet face-to-face with at least one woman who has been successfully treated for breast cancer. Find someone who has a positive attitude and who is a good listener. You might already know someone who fits that description, or your doctor can refer you to patients he or she has treated. Online conversations are well and good, but your computer can't give you a hug, hand you a Kleenex, or hold your hand.

Put Your Own Needs First

This really isn't as selfish as it sounds. In the long run, everybody will be better off because you took care of yourself when you needed to. Even so, it's difficult for many women to hand off their responsibilities. We are society's caretakers, its wives and mothers and usually its nurses, secretaries, child-care workers, and schoolteachers. We tend to put our loved ones' needs before our own. A breast cancer diagnosis can require a sudden reversal of lifelong habits, which will likely be yet another source of stress, at first.

Let people close to you be helpful. You don't have to be Superwoman. Explain to your family and friends that you must put all your energy into your treatment—not only surgery and therapies, but also learning, resting, and staying focused, which will help you keep your spirits up.

Minimize Outside Obligations

Life goes on, even if you aren't able to in your usual fashion. Some women continue with all their activities during breast cancer treatment; others decide to scale back a little, or a lot. You may need to rethink your professional and community responsibilities. If you serve on committees or boards, or lead a scout troop, or volunteer at a homeless shelter, or work outside the home, let people know that you'll be out of commission for a while and that someone else will have to fill in for you.

At your job, try to anticipate problems and prepare for them. Work with your employer to find a temporary replacement for the times you can't be there. Check to see how much sick leave you can take, what your employer's extended-leave policy is, and whether you have long-term-care insurance. You might not need a long absence from work, but it's good to know how to arrange one if necessary.

If your employer is uncooperative, remember that state laws and the federal Americans with Disabilities Act and Family Medical Leave Act exist to protect your job, your benefits, your seniority, and your status, and require your employer to provide "reasonable accommodation" to you during your treatment and recovery. These laws apply to most public agencies and all but the smallest private employers. (Some federal employees are covered by a different law.)

For details on your legal rights under state and federal law and to receive an informative booklet, contact the American Cancer Society (see the Resources section at the back of this book).

Being Involved in Your Treatment

The level of your involvement in your treatment really is up to you. The questions that are most important to you, and your urgency in getting them answered, will serve as a guide. Bit by bit, you'll discover whether you want detailed information about every procedure, medication, and treatment option, or whether you're content to know only enough to be an informed patient.

Take your time deciding how involved you want to be—then feel free to change your mind. Maybe at first you'll want to be a walking breast cancer encyclopedia, but later, after getting to know and trust your cancer specialist, decide you are satisfied with just a grasp of the general principles.

Emotional and Psychological Support

Think about coping strategies that have helped you keep your balance in the past. You can rely on this inner strength now. But if your coping skills aren't up to the task, your doctor, your research, and your support system can help.

It's natural to experience powerful and sometimes conflicting emotions after a diagnosis of breast cancer. Acknowledge your feelings and give them room. Confide in people who will listen and understand—even when your feelings are difficult to describe—and avoid well-meaning friends who try to talk you out of feeling the way you do.

Do not deny your emotions, no matter how inappropriate they might seem at first. Who knows? Tuning in to your most turbulent emotions, and surrendering to quietly pensive feelings as well, might surprise you with moments of great joy, even in the midst of sorrow and anger. Life warrants all these feelings, and more, and a crisis such as breast cancer can bring all of life into sharp focus.

Your goal of feeling strong and at peace is not well served if you explode in anger over small things, take your fears out on others, or pretend to be on top of things when you're not. As with most situations, a balanced and honest approach is the most effective.

Find creative ways to uncover and release your emotions. Writing, making music, dancing, drawing, painting, doing home-improvement projects, gardening, and even cooking can be excellent ways to express your feelings and create something worthwhile in the process. Conversation—intimate, confidential talk with your husband, partner, or a friend—can be healing and strengthening if that person is supportive.

If your emotions seem out of control, however, and nothing has helped, consider getting professional counseling. Ask your doctor to refer you to someone who specializes in working with cancer patients, especially women with breast cancer.

It's not that strong emotion is inappropriate. Tears and anger are normal and even healthy ways to keep from bottling up your feelings. Allow yourself to cry and grieve. Give yourself permission to be angry. As long as your anger isn't unleashed on them, the people who care about you should accept it and not scold you for "giving in to it." The most uncomfortable feelings of sadness and anger will be resolved sooner if you plod on through them rather than try to sneak around them.

Choose the appropriate time and place to punch pillows or shout yourself hoarse. Let your anger become the energy that pushes you to learn, take charge, take care of yourself, hang on to humor, and hope. But if, instead of *releasing* your anger, you end up feeling angrier than ever, consider it a sign that you could benefit from counseling or a therapeutic support group.

You might think the feelings that surge inside you have never been experienced by anyone else. The truth is, you're not alone. Others have felt, or are feeling right now, the very same emotions.

Support Groups

Other breast cancer patients can offer you validation and hope. They can understand your feelings and experiences. In fact, your support group might become vitally important, if only to relieve your feelings of isolation. Knowing you are not alone can give you great comfort.

Breast cancer support groups are made up of women of all ages and from all walks of life. Most large hospitals offer support groups specifically for women with breast cancer. Those who take advantage of them report that the meetings and the new relationships give them strength. Hearing others express fears, celebrate triumphs (large or small), and share valuable information can be healing and calming. Sadly, the women who could profit most from a support group—who are the most depressed, anxious, and fearful—often don't join one.

The National Cancer Institute's Cancer Information Service, the American Cancer Society, the Susan G. Komen Breast Cancer Foundation, and your hospital or breast cancer clinic can help you find appropriate support groups that meet face-to-face or online. The National Coalition for Cancer Survivorship helps cancer survivors and their families start local support groups or contact existing ones. For information about contacting these organizations, see the Resources section of this book.

I feel like I've been able to help others through my own breast cancer. All of my co-workers had mammograms right after I was diagnosed. One of them found she had a malignancy in the very early stages.

—Joan, 47

Spirituality

Some women already have strong religious faith or spirituality when they learn that they have breast cancer, or they soon find themselves drawn toward greater spirituality. Others rely on their own grit and self-reliance to see them through.

If you are spiritually inclined, your experience with breast cancer could deepen your faith. Talking with a minister, rabbi, priest, or other spiritual adviser about your illness may offer comfort. It can also become an opportunity to learn more about what you believe, what you fear, and what your particular faith teaches about God, mortality, the self, and the most satisfying way to live.

Most of these questions concern everyone, whether or not they profess religious faith, so they are worth your contemplation. If you are not religious, talking with those who are can be enlightening. You can also find wisdom in the works of nonreligious thinkers and in poetry, art, literature, and nature. Finding ways to look beyond the boundaries of your own life—perhaps seeing order and purpose there—can bring you peace and comfort. It is the kind of comfort that comes from feeling yourself small—not smaller than others, just part of an immense and very grand universe.

Meditation, Nutrition, and Exercise

One way to quiet your mind and relieve your anxiety is to meditate. Spending just ten to twenty minutes, twice a day, in a deeply relaxed and focused state not only confers a sense of tranquility but also helps the body fight the damaging effects of stress.

Some women meditate by silently repeating the word "peace" while calmly releasing any distractions that arise in the mind. Others use a form of meditation called *visualization* or *guided imagery*. In a state of deep relaxation, they picture the body healing itself. They intently visualize their cancer shrinking, their immune cells fighting like microscopic armies against cancer cells, their energy returning, their color radiant, their life in balance.

If meditation appeals to you, learn more about it through your research on the Internet or in publications. Consider taking a class in meditation or yoga. Some styles of yoga use stretches, movement, and body postures to promote a meditative state. Others focus more on yoga as exercise. Either can calm and energize you. In fact, any activity that lifts your spirits and supports your overall health will improve both your mental and physical well-being.

Eating healthfully is another way to fight your cancer. A nutritious low-fat diet has been shown to decrease the risk of getting cancer. Raw foods believed to inhibit cancer growth include broccoli, cabbage, brussels sprouts, cauliflower, mustard greens, turnip greens, kale, and radishes. Animal studies have demonstrated that dietary fiber can reduce the risk of breast cancer, perhaps by preventing estrogen from stimulating the growth of breast malignancies.

Other studies suggest that a diet high in the antioxidant vitamins A and C, as well as beta carotene (which the body converts to vitamin A), offers protection against cancer. Recent research has shown that vitamin D may provide protection from diseases such as cancer, osteoporosis, hypertension, and some auto- immune disease. Ask you doctor about the dosage that is right for you.

More than a hundred studies have found significant decreases in cancer rates among people whose diets are high in the fruits and vegetables that contain these vitamins. Good sources of beta carotene are apricots, beet greens, black-eyed peas, cantaloupe, carrots, sweet potatoes, pumpkin, and spinach. Studies have not confirmed the benefits of taking vitamin pills.

> ***When my mom first told me about her cancer, I was worried. Who would take care of me? What if she dies? She was totally honest with me. That was reassuring.***
>
> *—Gail 13*

Maximize the benefits of your low-fat, antioxidant-rich diet with exercise, which can improve both mental and physical health. Three to four hours of aerobic exercise a week will reduce your risk of cancer.

Addressing the Needs of Others

As much as you want to spare your family and friends any pain, worry, or inconvenience, in one way or another your breast cancer will affect everyone around you. Your husband or life partner, especially, is likely to experience intense emotions. Your children's reactions will depend on their age, personality, gender, and stage of emotional development. Your friends, especially women close to you in age, will not only be concerned about you but might also be somewhat anxious, knowing that they too could develop breast cancer.

Some people will know instinctively how to comfort you and offer help. Most will not, at least at first. Some never will be able to. There is no "right way" for someone to react to your illness. Try not to judge or be hurt when friends or relatives are awkward around you or even avoid you. It doesn't mean they don't care. It's just that everyone copes differently and expresses emotions in different ways.

After working with breast cancer patients for 14 years, I've found that patients connecting with other patients is the key to coping. Patients sharing their journeys is the best medicine.
—Ann, oncology social worker

Throughout your treatment, you'll naturally be concerned about the people close to you. Putting yourself first doesn't mean ignoring your friends and family, especially your children. Though most of your active care for others should wait until your treatments have ended, there are ways to help without immersing yourself in their difficulties.

The following sections describe what the people in your life might be going through and how you can acknowledge their struggles without letting them wear you down.

Spouses

If your spouse is the strong, silent type, he may hesitate to discuss his feelings for fear of burdening you. He might go into denial about your disease, or he might overcompensate by being excessively cheerful. The more you share your feelings and needs with him, the better he may be able to face his own. You might need to give him explicit permission to open up emotionally. But perhaps he can't do that, or provide the support you need, no matter how much he loves you. Sometimes people just get mired in feelings of fear, sadness, anger, or helplessness in the face of their partners' disease.

Letting him know that you don't blame him—and that you are not without support from friends, clergy, a counselor, or a support group—could help him deal with his own emotions. Eventually, he might learn how to help you by helping himself. Or he might not, in which case you can choose to accept him the way he is. The alternative—a constant, smoldering resentment—will be at least as harmful to you as to him.

Remind relatives and friends that they can make a world of difference by offering a kind word, babysitting, or otherwise sharing responsibility with your husband. Looking back, many husbands say they would simply like to have been asked, "How are *you* doing?"

If your husband, or anyone else, asks, "What can I do to help you?" take him up on the offer. Doing something constructive—some activity that will reduce your anxiety.

For a whole year, I woke up each morning and said to myself, 'You have breast cancer.' It was like being on an emotional roller coaster.
—Kristine, 51

Children

Children of every age, newborn to adult, are profoundly affected by a mother's breast cancer. Even infants are attuned to their parents' emotions and unsettled by the secrecy surrounding illness. The best thing you can do is accept their natural reactions to your cancer. Answer their questions with as much or as little information as they can absorb at their age and level of development. It might help them to confide in a trusted adult who isn't caught up in the crisis—a school counselor, teacher, neighbor, pastor, or friend.

Babies and Toddlers

The youngest children often respond to parents' stress by crying more, needing more attention, eating less, and sleeping poorly. Hold and comfort them as often as possible. Try to keep them on a consistent schedule. If they have begun to talk, give them very simple information ("Mommy's sick") and prepare them for changes in the household routine ("She might have to go away for a few days to get better").

Children Ages 3 to 6

At these ages, children do not yet have reasoning skills and can see things only from their own point of view. They might think they caused the cancer or they might worry about getting sick themselves. Since young children tend to fear separation, prepare them for your absences. When neither parent can be with them, they should be cared for (preferably at home, where they feel safe) by someone they know well and trust.

Because they don't understand their emotions, they might act out—throwing tantrums, hitting, pushing, crying. Try to maintain their daily routine. Calmly, in simple terms, explain any changes from that routine. Comfort them, reassure them that they are not at fault, and acknowledge that they might feel sad or scared.

I had friends who had breast cancer and they really got me through the tough times. I would lay out all my fears and one of them would always have something funny to say about it. We would just howl. It's hard to be afraid of something when you can laugh at it.
—Ann, 53

Children Ages 7 to 11

By this time, children are beginning to think logically. Capable of reasoning, they are also capable of understanding (and fearing) the finality of death. They'll be most anxious about the immediate future, however. They might worry about the tangible effects of your cancer, such as the cost of medical care or the welfare of younger siblings. Acknowledge their fears and other feelings, and assure them that adults have these matters well in hand.

Always be truthful, without giving them more information than they can grasp. If you can't promise you'll recover, give them realistic reasons for hope, such as treatment advances, new discoveries through research, and inspirational stories about women who have beaten the odds.

Adolescent Children

From 12 through their teenage years, children experience rapid physical, psychological, and emotional changes that make them extremely vulnerable. Because they are trying hard to establish their independence, develop their own identity, and separate from parents and childhood, they typically deny their vulnerability. Teenagers cling to self-absorption—the way a bud seems to hold itself tightly before it flowers—and think that bad things happen to other people, not to them.

Their mother's illness can undermine this certainty and draw them back into childhood and dependency. Be sensitive to this. Ask them to help out in tangible ways, recognizing that they are approaching adulthood but still have one foot in childhood. Talk about your own feelings in ways they can understand and deal with. This might prompt them to do likewise. But don't push. Sometimes, just being together is more reassuring than serious talk.

Adult Children

Your grown children will want to know how they can help, whether they live nearby or on another continent. No matter what their ages, a mother's serious illness can awaken long-forgotten feelings of dependence and deep anxiety, which may in turn trigger the need to control. A son, for example, who typically uses his competence to deal with uncertainty might want to take charge of your care. Welcome his concern, share information with him, but firmly assure him that you are capable of making all the necessary decisions. Daughters are likely to worry about their own susceptibility to breast cancer, as well they should. Emphasize the importance of monthly breast self-examination and annual checkups. Express the hope that your breast-cancer diagnosis will actually reduce their own risk by making them more conscientious about preventive care.

Other Family Members, Friends, and Acquaintances

Members of your extended family will naturally feel the impact of your cancer in different ways. Your parents may fear for you as they did when you were a child, and you might find your traditional roles turned upside-down as they look to you for comfort and reassurance.

Your siblings, besides being worried, will also feel a bit fragile themselves. If you are the first person of your generation to have cancer, they'll be awakened to their own vulnerability. If your cancer is hereditary, your sisters will have to confront their own breast cancer risk and that of their daughters. These concerns may seem selfish, but they may also be quite realistic and they certainly don't diminish your siblings' love for you or their compassion for your struggle.

Family and friends will deal with your illness in ways that reflect their personalities, character, emotional makeup, and just plain busy-ness. Don't be offended by those who don't call or visit as often as others or who are less forthcoming with food, favors, and willingness to sit and talk with you. Some people have no idea what to do or say. Let them know that you understand, that it helps just to know they care, and that you're still interested in their day-to-day goings-on. Your reassurance might free them to show their concern more openly.

Sexuality and Intimacy

There's no medical reason to delay having sex after breast surgery unless your doctor advises otherwise. But you might not be particularly interested in sex right away, for a variety of reasons. For one thing, you've just had surgery and you'll be gathering your strength for a while. On top of that, your nonsurgical therapy—radiation, chemotherapy, hormonal therapy, or another treatment—can temporarily dampen your desire, tire you, or cause other symptoms (such as vaginal dryness) that are likely to bump sexual activity off the top of your priority list.

After a mastectomy, with or without breast reconstruction, you have an entirely new body image to adjust to, and it will take some time for you to feel sexy and appealing. And at the same time, you're fearing your partner's reaction to your altered anatomy, he might be reluctant to approach you for fear of causing you physical pain. But if you're not communicating, it's easy to draw the wrong conclusions, each of you perhaps thinking the other is indifferent.

For some couples, unacknowledged barriers to intimacy are a serious threat to the relationship. A discussion with your doctor might be helpful for the two of you. The doctor can explain to what extent your problem might be physiological, caused by treatment-induced hormonal changes, and to what extent it is emotional. He or she can reassure your partner that having sex won't cause you physical injury. And your doctor or a counselor can open the lines of communication between the two of you. For clearly, communication is crucial here. If the two of you don't share your fears openly, there's a lot of room for misunderstanding. Keeping quiet about anxieties will only push them deeper.

Assure your partner that you find him desirable. Tell him about your insecurities, and encourage him to share his feelings as well. Most husbands prove to be loving, supportive, and accepting of their wives' changed bodies and their topsy-turvy feelings.

My doctor found my breast cancer during a routine mammogram shortly after I turned 40. I immediately started to cry and thought I was going to die, but I didn't.

—Alice, 46

Until you are energetic and confident enough to have intercourse, you can maintain closeness by cuddling, holding, caressing, and confiding in one another. Without question, do not have sex until you're ready. Experts are unanimous on this point: Feeling obligated to have intercourse when you'd rather be doing almost anything else can be an ever-present source of stress and guilt feelings, which aren't beneficial at any time but can be especially harmful to you now. Allow time for your body and spirit to heal, and look forward to a lifetime of growing, changing, and maturing intimacy with the one you love.

4

Surgery for Breast Cancer

Virtually every woman diagnosed with breast cancer undergoes surgery, which may or may not be followed by radiation and other therapies. Today, women with breast cancer can choose from a variety of surgical options that were not available to their mothers. This is good news. Modern surgical techniques have increased survival rates and helped many women avoid losing one or both breasts. Yet the array of options can make it more difficult to weigh the relative advantages and disadvantages. Many women feel overwhelmed by unfamiliar medical terms and decisions to make at a time when they are already emotionally overwrought. They may feel their very lives depend on the right choice, and yet they also feel numb, unable to focus or make sense of things just when the need for clarity is great.

For this reason, it's a good idea to take your partner or a close friend with you when you first meet with your surgeon. Have your companion take notes or tape-record these conversations so that you need not grasp and remember all the new information laid out before you. Later, you and your companion can talk everything over.

Choosing a Breast Surgeon

After a breast cancer diagnosis, your doctor will likely refer you to a breast surgeon. If you like and trust the breast surgeon to whom your doctor has referred you, great! If not, perhaps you'll want to find the surgeon who is right for you. How do you go about this?

- Ask your physician for another referral.
- Get the names of breast cancer surgeons in your area from several credible sources: clergy, friends, co-workers, physicians, nurses, and other health professionals. Find out which of these surgeons are on the staffs of highly rated hospitals. Develop a working list, then look at the doctors' credentials on their Web sites. Interview as many as it takes to find one whom you trust and feel comfortable with.
- Get in touch with an organization such as the National Alliance of Breast Cancer Organizations (NABCO), the National Cancer Institute (NCI), the American Cancer Society, or the American Society of Breast Surgeons. Contact information for these and other organizations appears in the Resources section at the back of this book.
- Find breast-cancer hotlines or women's health groups in your area that can point you toward breast-cancer specialists and other resources.
- If you're involved in a support group or online chat room, ask other members how they went about their own searches.

Once you have found the right surgeon, he or she can refer you to other specialists, such as a radiation oncologist, who oversees radiation therapy or a medical oncologist, who oversees any type of chemotherapy. As before, you don't have to accept the surgeon's recommendations and may wish to evaluate each doctor on your own.

In general, a doctor who is ethical, experienced, and attuned to your needs is one who:

- shows genuine concern for you and is not overly clinical or detached

- is a good teacher, explaining things thoroughly but clearly, in language you can readily understand
- takes a detailed history and performs a complete physical exam
- asks how you're feeling emotionally, who is helping you through your crisis, and whether you have or need a support group
- gives you a realistic picture of your illness and outlook but is calm and reassuring
- has considerable experience with cases like yours
- is up-to-date on the newest treatments and research
- welcomes the involvement of family members or a close friend
- supports the use of all necessary pain control
- patiently answers all your questions and does not regard any of them as unimportant
- notices when you're confused or anxious and tactfully draws you out
- encourages you to get a second opinion on any treatment decision

Before Surgery

You will no doubt have questions about your surgery. When it comes to your breast cancer and its treatments, there's no such thing as an inappropriate question. Ask your doctor *before* you check in for surgery about anything that concerns you, though it might not be possible to answer some of your questions until after surgery. Here are some sample questions to help you start your own list:

- Will I need radiation therapy, chemotherapy, hormonal therapy, or targeted therapy following my surgery?
- When is breast reconstruction safer—at the time of surgery, or later? Which do you recommend?
- What side effects can I expect from surgery?

- Will my surgery be done on an outpatient basis, or will I be hospitalized? If so, for how long?
- Where will my surgical incisions be? What will my scars look like?
- Will I have drainage tubes?
- When will I be able to go back to work?
- Will my physical activities be restricted? For how long?
- Will I need physical therapy?

Surgical Incisions and Scars

Before your breast surgery, talk with your surgeon about the incision or incisions that will be used. If you are having a partial mastectomy, you will want to know how much scarring to expect and how the surgeon will keep scarring to a minimum. The shape and direction of the incision can influence whether your remaining breast tissue will pucker, whether your scar will draw the nipple out of its normal position or show above a bathing suit, and whether your breast will have any concave areas.

If your entire breast will be removed and you want to have reconstruction, ask how much of your skin can be spared for the process and how the incision will be positioned to allow for the best cosmetic outcome.

Techniques for hiding or minimizing scars are continually improving. For example, since the nipple position and weight distribution are completely different in upright positions, surgeons now decide on placement of incisions based on the appearance of a woman's breasts when she is standing, sitting, and walking, rather than during an examination, when she is lying down.

Types of Breast Surgery

The type of breast surgery your surgeon recommends depends on several factors, including the type, stage, and location of the cancer; your feelings about breast preservation or reconstruction; your prognosis; and your general health.

Overall, breast surgery is straightforward, and complications are rare. Hospital stays depend on the surgery being performed and whether any reconstruction will be done. Most stays are overnight; longer stays—two to six days—are sometimes needed if reconstruction is done immediately after the cancer surgery.

Partial Mastectomy

When a portion of the breast is removed during surgery, the procedure is called a *partial mastectomy*. There are two major types of partial mastectomy—lumpectomy and *quadrantectomy*. The difference between them is the amount of the breast that is removed. Partial mastectomies are usually outpatient procedures, even with lymph node removal.

Lumpectomy

Also known as *breast conserving therapy (BCT)*, a lumpectomy removes the tumor and some of the surrounding healthy tissue. This procedure is possible when a tumor is small, easy to access, and situated so that a complete margin of healthy tissue can be taken and analyzed. The *margin* is the border of normal tissue remaining around the tumor that has been removed. A wide margin that is clear of cancer indicates that the entire tumor has most likely been removed and the chance of a local recurrence (cancer returning to the same site) is low.

Quadrantectomy

A *quadrantectomy* removes all or most of one quadrant of the breast, including the skin and connective tissue, and sometimes the underarm lymph nodes. A *quadrant,* which represents about one-fourth of the breast, is not an anatomical reality but simply a figurative way of referring to areas of the breast.

Quadrantectomy may be the best choice when the tumor is large or the breast is small, or both, so that removing the tumor and adequate margins requires removal of a sizable part of the breast. After surgery, the affected breast might be noticeably smaller than the healthy one. Follow-up surgery can equalize breast size and restore symmetry, either by enlarging the smaller breast or reducing the larger one.

For most early-stage breast cancers, lumpectomy includes biopsy of the lymph nodes and is nearly always followed by radiation. The combination of lumpectomy and radiation is as effective as mastectomy. This is a great blessing for women who are especially apprehensive about losing a breast.

For the preinvasive condition ductal carcinoma in situ (DCIS), partial mastectomy is often performed to remove the malignant cell clusters that are otherwise likely to invade surrounding tissues.

Confer with your surgeon about the advantages and disadvantages of lumpectomy and quadrantectomy in your situation.

Total Mastectomy

Total mastectomy, also called *simple mastectomy,* removes the entire breast; sometimes the nipple can be saved. No lymph nodes are removed, although a separate sentinel node biopsy, remov-

Quadrantectomy

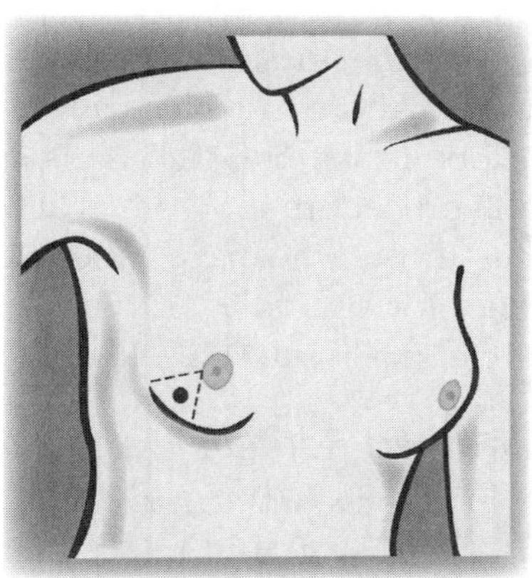

When doing a partial mastectomy, the surgeon removes the tumor, some surrounding breast tissue, and the lining over the chest muscles.

Lumpectomy

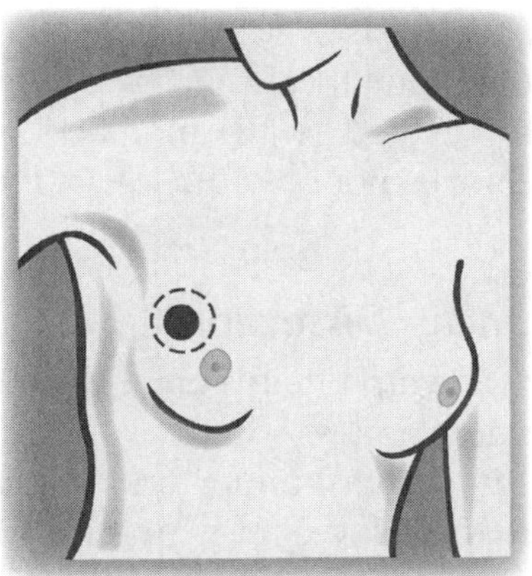

In a lumpectomy procedure, the lump and surrounding tissue are removed.

ing the first one to three axillary lymph nodes, may also be performed.

Simple mastectomy is often performed for *multifocal* breast cancers, those in which cancer is detected in more than one duct or lobe in the breast. It is also an effective *prophylactic* (preventive) procedure for women at high risk for aggressive breast cancer—those who have inherited an abnormal BRCA1 or BRCA2 gene, for example, or who have been diagnosed with lobular carcinoma in situ (LCIS).

Modified Radical Mastectomy

The *modified radical mastectomy,* an older approach to breast removal and rarely performed today, removes all breast tissue, covering an area from the breastbone to the back of the armpit and from the collarbone to the lower bra line, and some or all of the axillary lymph nodes. Occasionally, the small strap-like pectoralis minor muscle above the breast is removed if it interferes with node removal or if it has been invaded by cancer cells. Today, however, since the vast majority of breast cancers are discovered before they invade the chest muscles, the cancer can be removed using simpler, less invasive surgery.

The modified radical mastectomy is performed when the cancer's size, stage, or location rules out partial mastectomy. Some multifocal cancers and most stage III and stage IV cancers are treated with modified radical mastectomy, because it removes not only the breast tissue but also the cancerous lymph nodes.

Axillary Dissection

Lymph fluid from the breast and arm drains into the axillary lymph nodes, so any cancer cells that are beginning to spread from a breast tumor usually show up first in these nodes. There are three levels of lymph nodes in the axillary region, extending in an uneven line from below the armpit to the upper chest, near the collarbone. Because the lymph nodes are surrounded by fat pads and connective tissue, and because the number of nodes at each level varies, it can be difficult to locate every single node when searching for cancer.

In a surgical procedure called *axillary dissection,* once routinely performed as part of a mastectomy or partial mastectomy, the surgeon removes level I and II lymph nodes and purposely avoids removing level III nodes. The nodes are sent to a pathologist for immediate analysis. The more nodes removed, the less likely that hard-to-locate nodes, any of which can contain cancer cells, will be overlooked. But the lymph nodes are there for a reason, and removal of most or all of them can cause *lymphedema*—a painful swelling described later in this chapter.

Sentinel Node Biopsy

Axillary dissection became much less common with the earlier diagnosis of breast cancer and the advent of the *sentinel node biopsy.* In fact, sentinel node biopsy is now the standard technique for finding and measuring the spread of breast cancer into the lymph nodes.

This procedure involves sampling a single axillary node

Total Mastectomy

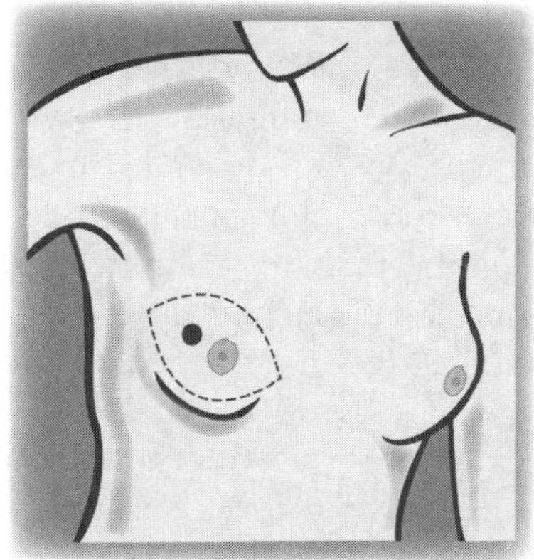

In a total (simple) mastectomy procedure, the entire breast is removed, but no lymph nodes are removed.

Modified Radical Mastectomy

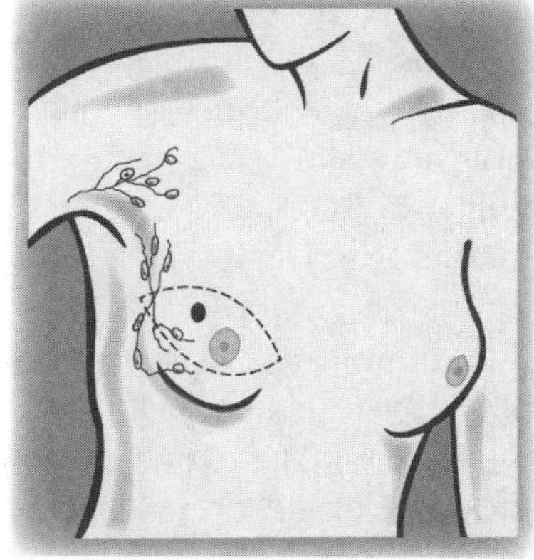

A modified radical mastectomy involves removing the entire breast, and all breast tissue extending toward the breastbone, collarbone, and to the lowest ribs; also lymph nodes in the armpit are removed and sometimes the minor pectoral muscle.

called the *sentinel node,* which is usually the first to receive lymph drainage from the tumor area and therefore the first in which a spreading cancer is likely to show up. The surgeon finds the sentinel node by injecting a blue dye, a radioactive tracer, or both near the tumor. These substances show up clearly on a hand-held monitor called a *scintillator,* so the surgeon can see the path they take from the tumor to the lymph nodes. The first node reached by the dye and/or tracer is the sentinel node. The surgeon removes that node and it is examined under a microscope. Removing only one node or a few is a much less extensive procedure than removing all or most of the nodes; further, this procedure is much less likely to result in the development of lymphedema.

Only if cancer is found in the sentinel node are the other nodes removed, since cancer may be present in them as well. The sentinel node can also be analyzed without surgery by needle biopsy.

Post-Surgical Drains

Immediately after a mastectomy or axillary dissection, the surgeon may place soft plastic tubes, or *drains,* under the skin near the closed incision. The tubes prevent discomfort and possibly infection by carrying away the tissue fluid that builds up while the incision is healing. There might be some blood in this fluid at first, but it will soon run pale yellow, collecting in a small bulb at the end of each tube. The drains are removed when the fluid diminishes, usually after five to seven days.

Let your doctor know immediately about any severe pain, which could be a sign of *hematoma,* blood pooling in tissue at the surgical site, or internal bleeding.

Postsurgical Pain Management

Lumpectomy and mastectomy aren't generally associated with intense post-operative pain; however, managing any pain after breast surgery is essential to your comfort and to the healing process. With discomfort at a minimum, you're better able to get the rest you need to recover. Several pain management options are available during your hospital stay and during your recovery at home. Depending on your procedure, your post-surgical pain-relief options while in the hospital may include pain relieving drugs, which are delivered through an intravenous line, patient-controlled analgesia (PCA), and the newer "pain relief ball." Pain relievers in pill form may also be given in the hospital or taken later at home.

Intravenous (IV) Pain Medication

A common pain management method used in hospitals following breast surgery is IV pain medication. With this method, opioid medications, such as morphine or Demerol, are delivered to you through your IV line. A nurse administers the medication at prescribed intervals, approximately every four hours. If you should continue to experience pain, notify your nurse, who may either administer another dose or consult with your surgeon about adjusting the dosage.

> ***I had a double mastectomy and was surprised that I had very little pain. Actually, the hardest part for me was losing my hair during chemotherapy.***
> ***—Shirley, 58***

Patient-Controlled Analgesia (PCA)

During a hospital stay, pain relief may be administered through *patient-controlled analgesia (PCA).* With PCA, pain medications, such as morphine, Demerol, or Dilaudid, are delivered through your intravenous line. The IV line is attached to a computerized pump that is usually mounted on a pole near your bed. When you feel pain, you simply press a button to activate the pump, which delivers a dose of medication. The pump is calibrated so that it is impossible to give yourself too many dosages.

It's usually best to give yourself small, frequent doses of the pain medication to provide steady relief. Waiting until your pain gets worse is not advisable and may make it more difficult for you to get comfortable again.

Pain Relief Ball

A newer pain management option used during a hospital stay is the ON-Q pain relief system, commonly called a "pain relief ball." At the end of a breast operation, the surgeon inserts a small catheter into the incision site; this catheter delivers a continuous infusion of local anesthetic. The catheter is attached to a small ball, a high-tech balloon filled with anesthetic. The system infuses anesthetic directly into the surgical site for up to five days, providing ongoing pain relief. The pain relief ball reduces the incidence of breakthrough pain and reduces the need for narcotic medications, which usually cause drowsiness and decreased mental alertness.

Opioid Medications

Opioid medications, also called narcotics or opiates, are commonly taken in pill form and are used to alleviate moderate to severe pain in the days following a mastectomy or lumpectomy. However, many women find that they need the medication for only a few days, if any, following surgery.

Opioids are associated with certain side effects, including nausea, sleepiness, constipation, and slowed breathing. Opioids commonly given during a hospital stay include morphine and Demerol. Commonly prescribed opioids for use at home include Tylenol with codeine, Vicodin, Percocet, and Darvocet. Although these medications can be habit-forming, they will not lead to addiction when taken for short periods of time. The drugs can be obtained only through a physician's prescription.

Nonopioid Medications

Nonopioid pain relievers are nonnarcotic, and many of them do not require a doctor's prescription. Designed to control mild to moderate pain, these medications include acetaminophen and nonsteroidal anti-inflammatory drugs (NSAIDs), such as ibuprofen and naproxen. Even though these drugs may not require a prescription, it's important to check with your doctor before taking them. Side effects are rarely associated with acetaminophen when taken for short periods. NSAIDs, however, can cause stomach pain, heartburn, dizziness, and constipation. Inform your doctor if you experience any side effects.

Recovery after Breast Surgery

Once your breast surgery is over, your recovery begins. Recovery from lumpectomy is relatively quick. However, recovery from mastectomy or mastectomy with lymph node removal requires more time, and complete recovery may take six to eight weeks. No matter which kind of surgery you've had, you'll notice improvement with each passing day.

If you've had a lumpectomy, you can expect to return to normal activities, such as walking, showering, and driving, within a day or two. Most women feel well enough to return to work within a few days. If you have had a sentinel node biopsy as part of your lumpectomy, it make take a few extra days before you're ready to return to work and other normal activities.

If you've had a mastectomy, it will be a week or more before you're ready to return to normal activities. If you've had a mastectomy with lymph node removal, you're likely to need some assistance with everyday tasks, such as washing your hair or caring for your children. Following mastectomy with or without lymph node removal, your return to work depends in part on the type of work you do.

If you have an office job, you'll be able to return to work sooner than if your work involves heavy lifting or strenuous labor. Some women return to work within a week; others take two or more weeks before going back to work.

Possible Side Effects of Surgery

Hematoma

A hematoma is a potential postsurgical complication that occurs when blood pools at the surgery site as a result of a leaking or ruptured blood vessel. Hematomas that occur in the breast after surgery may feel like a lump and may be painful. It is important to report this to your surgeon right away since a hematoma can cause tissue death in the area in which the bleeding occurs.

Anxiety and Depression

Some women are depressed after even the most successful surgery. Your body's response to the trauma of surgery can make you sad or anxious, as can the mental stress of a cancer diagnosis.

If you had a mastectomy, your first look at the place where your breast used to be may be difficult. You might even be a little afraid of seeing the surgery site after the bandages are removed. But putting it off will only create greater anxiety. When the time comes, you might want your partner or close friend there to "hold your hand."

Many women actually aren't as upset over their appearance after having had a breast removed as they expected to be. Relief that the tumor is gone usually outweighs their distress about scarring and even their very natural grief over losing a breast.

Restricted Arm Mobility and Numbness

If your lymph nodes were removed, your arm may be stiff for a few days to a few weeks. Physical therapy can help. You'll probably be shown some easy stretching and pulling exercises that will immediately improve your mobility. Eventually you'll have full, normal use of your arm. Even if small portions of muscle have been removed, your strength will return.

During lymph node removal, a skin nerve may have been cut. This is normal and not a cause for worry, though it can cause some unpleasant symptoms. Your upper arm might be numb, and starting a few days after the operation, you may feel tingling, sharp pains, or squeezing pressure. These sensations will go away in a week or two, although in a few cases (2 to 3 percent) a chronic ache remains.

Phantom Breast

Up to 80 percent of women who have had a mastectomy report that they can "feel" the missing breast, much as people "feel" a limb that has been amputated. If your breast tumor was painful, you might feel the "ghost" of that pain for weeks or months after your surgery. Some women have "phantom breast" sensations on and off for years—not painful, simply *there*. These sensations are being recalled by the brain, which does not forget. They do not mean the cancer has returned. Nevertheless, it is important to check with your doctor if any new or unusual pain begins, one that has not already been identified as a phantom sensation.

Lymphedema

If your arm should become inflamed—brought on by anything from a mosquito bite to a strained muscle—your body sends extra lymph fluid, which carries infection-fighting white blood cells, to the site of the inflammation. But if the lymph nodes and vessels have been removed from that side of your body, they're no longer available to drain away excess lymph. With nowhere to go, the fluid collects in your arm, causing it to swell.

Have someone with you before and after your surgery. My 80-year-old mother was with me and she kept saying she felt so useless because she couldn't do any housework or laundry for me. But she didn't realize what a help she was just by being there. It made a total difference.

—Marie, 45

This condition, called lymphedema, occurs in up to 20 percent of women who have had axillary dissection. The risk of lymphedema is lowest with sentinel-node biopsy and highest with complete axillary dissection.

Lymphedema is not life-threatening, but it can be painful and needs prompt treatment. If the symptoms are ignored, the fluid can become infected and, in severe cases, there can be permanent damage to the arm.

Because you can develop lymphedema anytime, even years after your surgery, you'll need to make prevention a lifelong regimen. This means maintaining a healthy weight and avoiding injury, infection, constriction, muscle strain, and temperature extremes, starting immediately after your surgery.

Call your doctor right away if you have swelling or pain in your arm; if an injury becomes puffy or tender; if your skin feels hot or is inflamed in any way—a rash, itching, or redness—or if you have a fever or flulike symptoms. Antibiotics and diuretics, given early on, can help, as can physical therapy and specialized massages given by a lymphedema therapist.

For more information about lymphedema, contact the National Lymphedema Network, listed in the Resources section at the back of this book.

Infection

If you notice even a slight swelling of your affected arm soon after mastectomy, or if swelling, redness, or warmth occurs under the incision, it could be a sign of infection. Notify your doctor immediately. Such infections can be serious and should be treated without delay.

Post-Surgical Prognosis

After your surgery, when the pathologist has examined the tumor and other tissues that were removed, your doctor will have a better idea about the need for additional treatment. The best possible news would be that the entire tumor and a clear margin have been removed, lymph-node analysis shows no cancer cells, and you can expect a full recovery.

The majority of women with breast cancer are cured. Even so, you'll need close follow-up, since not even the best outcome can guarantee that every cancer cell is gone or that cancer will not return. Getting rid of remaining cancer after surgery is the purpose of *adjuvant therapy*—treatment given after the primary treatment (surgery, in this case) to improve the chance for a cure. Adjuvant therapy may be *local*—for example, radiation directed at the cancer site—or *systemic,* affecting the entire body,

Tips for Preventing Lymphedema

- Lift nothing heavier than ten pounds with the affected arm while you're healing.
- Any exercise program or physical activity involving the arm should begin gradually and include frequent rest breaks.
- Get in the habit of consistent low-impact exercise, such as walking, swimming, or stretching.
- Don't carry a heavy purse over the affected shoulder.
- Be very protective of the affected arm to avoid injury that could lead to infection. Keep it clean. Use sunscreen and insect repellent. Use moisturizer to avoid chapping and cuticle cream to avoid hangnails (and don't cut your cuticles). Use an electric shaver, not a razor, to shave your underarms; don't use chemical hair removers. Protect your hands and arms when cooking or taking food out of a hot oven. Wear protective gloves for gardening and yard work, and rubber gloves when you're cleaning with chemicals and doing the dishes.
- Ask medical personnel not to use the affected arm to take your blood pressure, draw blood, or give an injection.
- If you get even a tiny cut or puncture, wash it with soap and water, apply an antibacterial ointment, and keep an eye on it for signs of infection.
- If you plan to take a long trip by air, consider wearing a compression garment to keep swelling down. Compression garments are sold online, in mail-order catalogs, and at many pharmacies. If you need a professionally fitted or custom-fitted compression garment, ask your doctor where you can obtain one in your area.
- Ask your doctor or a physical therapist for post-mastectomy exercises you can do to reduce the risk of lymphedema.

as with chemotherapy and hormone-blocking and targeted therapies.

If lymph nodes removed during surgery test positive for cancer or if your cancer was of a comparatively rare type that has a high risk of recurrence, your doctor will prescribe one or more forms of adjuvant therapy. If your tumor was *node-negative* (that is, with no cancer found in the lymph nodes), the doctor will probably order more tests to find out if you could benefit from adjuvant therapies as protection against recurrence.

The long-term outlook—your prognosis—depends on many factors, including your overall health, your individual anatomy, and your responses to therapy. Thus, your doctors will not be able to guarantee a particular prognosis. At best, they can tell you about general patterns of recovery, or recurrence in cases similar to yours.

However, no two cases are exactly alike. Many women meet bad news with a positive attitude and live longer than their prognosis seemed to predict. Meanwhile, new discoveries and treatments continually emerge, lengthening lives and instantly making older statistics obsolete. Continuing developments in therapy hold great promise for breast cancer patients.

5

Breast Reconstruction

It has been said that mastectomy treats the disease and reconstruction heals the mind. For women with breast cancer, treating the disease is the first and by far the most important consideration. Breast reconstruction is often a close second. You may be among the many women who, though forever grateful for their recovery from breast cancer, welcome the possibility of restoring the appearance of a natural breast in place of the one that was lost.

Breast reconstruction is a safe and effective option for almost any woman who has had a breast removed. In many cases, it can be done either at the time of her original breast surgery or later—even years later. Breast cancer treatment centers offer a comprehensive team approach involving a mastectomy surgeon, a reconstructive surgeon, physicians who specialize in chemotherapy and radiation, and skilled support personnel.

Is Breast Reconstruction Right for You?

The choice is intensely personal. Many women feel strong and confident without reconstruction. Much depends on your lifestyle, profession, and personal style.

An external prosthesis is an excellent alternative for women who can't have or don't want reconstruction. Today's prostheses are lighter and less bulky than the older types, and you can start wearing a prosthesis when you have healed sufficiently, often as soon as six weeks after your mastectomy. The breast-form materials can vary from silicone gel to fiberfill. Some types are made to fit into the pockets of post-mastectomy bras; others adhere directly to the chest.

Women who choose reconstruction, however, care about more than the way they look when fully clothed. Their breasts may be important to their sexuality, confidence, and feeling of femininity. They want to feel whole as well as look whole—they want to shower, dress, walk, reach, and bend with two breasts in place. And for some women, the mastectomy scar can be an ever-present reminder of their cancer, and reconstruction is a way to put it behind them.

Choosing a Plastic Surgeon

If you are considering breast reconstruction, make an appointment with a plastic surgeon who specializes in breast reconstruction. It is important that you feel comfortable with the surgeon and confident that you can communicate openly with him or her from the time of your first consultation to your follow-up care. Be forthright with your questions. Ask about the various reconstruction procedures available and which one he or she would advise for you. Ask to see photographs of reconstructions the plastic surgeon has performed and to be put in touch with patients who have had similar procedures.

It is also important that the surgeon be board-certified. Being board-certified means that a plastic surgeon has participated in a residency program in both general surgery and plastic surgery and has passed comprehensive written and oral exams. Then, board certification is granted by the American Board of Plastic Surgery (ABPS).

Plastic surgeons who have earned board certification are required to be recertified every ten years. To qualify for recertification, surgeons must receive additional training on a regular basis. This is often achieved by participating in continuing medical education. In addition, surgeons must continually meet the moral and ethical standards set by the ABPS.

The Reconstruction Plan

In a breast-reconstruction procedure, the surgeon creates a breast mound as much like the natural breast as possible. The goal of breast reconstruction is to restore symmetry or evenness to the chest wall. But if only one breast is reconstructed, no matter how realistic it is, it won't look exactly like the natural breast. Thus, many women choose to modify the natural breast with an implant, reduction, or lift, so that it more closely resembles the reconstructed breast.

Breast reconstruction should never be allowed to interfere with your number-one priority—eliminating cancer from your body. Thus, the timing and technique of your surgery will depend on the scheduling of any additional treatment, such as radiation or chemotherapy.

Immediate or Delayed Reconstruction?

Don't feel pressured to make up your mind about reconstruction before your breast surgery. As mentioned earlier, you can choose reconstruction at any time. If you know ahead of time that you will want reconstruction, you and your doctor will decide when you will have it—at the time of your breast surgery, or later. There are, however, advantages to having immediate reconstruction.

I kept a journal through my breast cancer experience to remember things so I could help others. The day of my surgery, I gave my journal to my friends and family who were with me in the hospital, and they wrote their thoughts. Those have been the pages I have read the most.

—Marilyn, 61

- *Financial*: It costs less to have the mastectomy and the reconstruction in the same surgery than to have the procedures at different times.
- *Emotional/Psychological*: Immediate reconstruction eliminates two sources of distress—a second surgery later on, and the experience of waking from the first surgery with no breast.

- *Personal*: Some women who would be candidates for lumpectomy with radiation therapy choose instead to have mastectomy with immediate reconstruction in order to avoid radiation.
- *Geographic*: Women in rural areas where radiation is not locally available may choose mastectomy with immediate reconstruction over lumpectomy followed by radiation.
- *Practical*: Women with jobs outside the home can minimize their time away from work by consolidating the two surgeries. Stay-at-home moms won't have to arrange child care around two operations.
- *Cosmetic*: In some cases, immediate reconstruction gives a better cosmetic result.

Not every woman is a candidate for immediate reconstruction. Radiation sometimes (but not always) makes it necessary to postpone reconstruction. Delaying the procedure might also be advised for patients with advanced breast cancer.

Women whose general health is poor or who are having emotional problems are usually better off postponing reconstruction. The best time to have reconstructive surgery is *not* when you are in the middle of a financial crisis, divorce, or bereavement.

Delaying reconstruction gives you time to think and become informed. The decision-making process for breast surgery alone can be overwhelming. By putting off reconstruction, you can weigh your options carefully, recover from your mastectomy, and find out whether you even want or need reconstruction.

Reconstruction Options

There are several surgical options for breast reconstruction. With every option, it is important to weigh the advantages and disadvantages of both the procedure and its outcomes. Whichever method is used, the opposite breast is usually modified for the sake of symmetry, most commonly with a breast lift and sometimes with breast reduction or breast augmentation.

Reconstruction with Implants

The most common type of reconstruction uses an implant to create a breast mound. In some cases, implant reconstruction can be performed as a single-stage procedure with an implant being placed in the breast during the mastectomy procedure. In most cases, however, implant reconstruction is a two-stage process. The first stage involves the placement of a tissue expander, which can be performed immediately during your mastectomy procedure or can be delayed until several months or even years later. The second stage involves replacing the tissue expander with an implant.

There are several advantages associated with reconstruction using an implant. The procedure is considered relatively simple compared to other reconstruction methods. The surgeon almost always inserts the implant using the same incision that was used for the mastectomy, which means there are no additional resulting scars. Because the surgery is limited to the breast area, recovery is quicker than with other types of reconstruction.

Implant

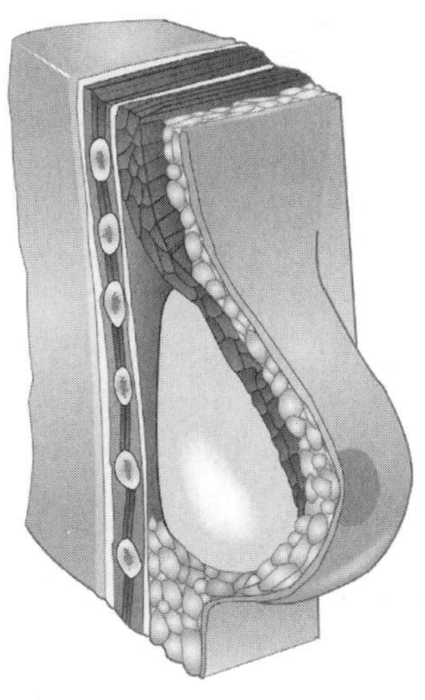

An implant is the most common method of breast reconstruction. Typically, a tissue expander, filled gradually with saline, is used to stretch the skin so it will accommodate the insertion of an implant.

This reconstruction method also has its disadvantages. Implants may feel firmer than a natural breast, and symmetry may be difficult to achieve unless the other breast is modified in some way. Also, the implant will retain its shape and firmness over the years while the natural breast ages. The difference isn't generally apparent under clothing, and products called *symmetry shapers* or *balance shapers* can be tucked into the bra to even out the appearance of the breasts.

In some instances, implant reconstruction may not be right for you. If you've had radiation therapy, your skin may not have enough elasticity to be stretched adequately to accommodate an implant. Likewise, if the skin and tissue in the breast area are considered poor quality, implant surgery may not be recommended.

Stage 1: Tissue Expansion

In most cases, the first stage of implant reconstruction is *tissue expansion*, a gradual stretching of the skin and chest muscle to create a pocket for the permanent implant. At the time of your mastectomy, or in a later procedure if you are delaying reconstruction, the surgeon places a tissue expander—a temporary balloon-like device made of elastic silicone rubber—under the skin and chest muscle. Whether a tissue expander is placed at the same time as a mastectomy or in a delayed procedure, it takes approximately one to two hours. In a delayed procedure, tissue expander placement is performed using anesthesia in an operating room. The procedure may be performed on an outpatient basis, or it may require a brief hospital stay.

Approximately once every one to two weeks for two to four months, fluid is injected through a port, or entry site, that is part of the tissue expander itself or connected to a tube just under the skin. Gradually, the volume of fluid grows, the skin and muscle expand, and the pocket is created.

If you are scheduled for radiation and you are planning to undergo tissue expansion, it's recommended to have tissue expansion performed prior to beginning radiation treatments. That's because, as mentioned above, radiated skin loses its elasticity and is unable to be stretched. Once you've completed radiation treatment, your surgeon will evaluate the skin in your breast area to determine if you're a candidate for implant placement. If not, having undergone tissue expansion can still be beneficial; it can give the surgeon greater latitude in shaping your new breast using other types of reconstruction.

During tissue expansion, you may notice some discomfort for a day or so after each injection; what you're feeling is the muscle stretching to accommodate the additional fluid. Your surgeon can prescribe pain medication if necessary, but many women alleviate any discomfort with over-the-counter medications.

Stage 2: Implant Placement

Whether an implant is placed at the same time as a mastectomy or following tissue expansion, it takes approximately one to two hours. Implant placement following tissue expansion can be performed using anesthesia on an outpatient basis, or it may require a hospital stay of one to two days. During the procedure, your doctor will remove the tissue expander, insert the permanent implant, and modify (lift, augment, or reduce) the opposite breast for symmetry or evenness.

> ***I was able to get through my reconstruction by telling myself, 'You can do this. You're going to look great when it's over!'***
>
> *—Joan, 47*

For breast reconstruction, implants are almost always placed submuscularly, under the pectoral muscle. It's possible for an implant to be placed above the muscle, but since there is no breast tissue to cover it, the implant may be easy to feel and may not appear natural-looking. Submuscular placement generally provides a more natural look and feel.

Types of Implants

The implants used in reconstruction consist of a silicone shell and are filled with either saline or silicone gel. Saline implants are filled with sterile saline, a saltwater solution similar to the body's own fluids. If a saline implant leaks or ruptures, the saline is absorbed by the body and eliminated through urination. Silicone gel is denser than saline, and many surgeons and women believe that silicone implants look and feel more

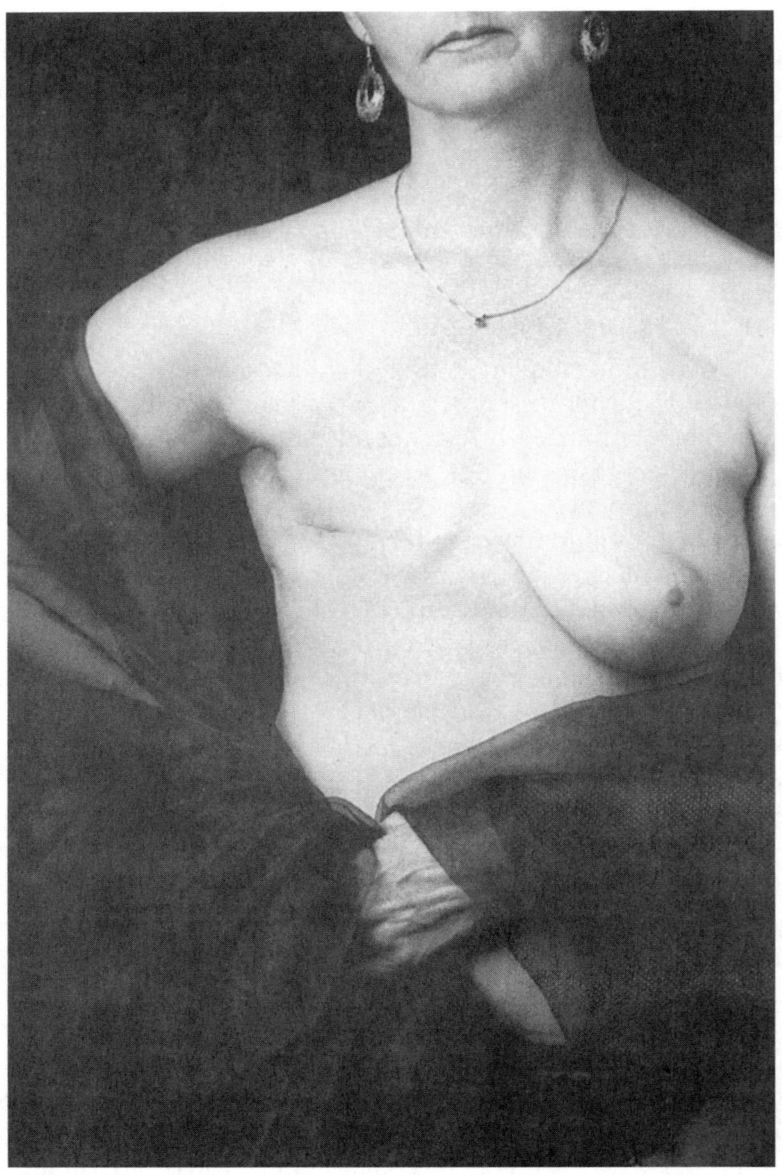

This woman had a mastectomy at age 43.

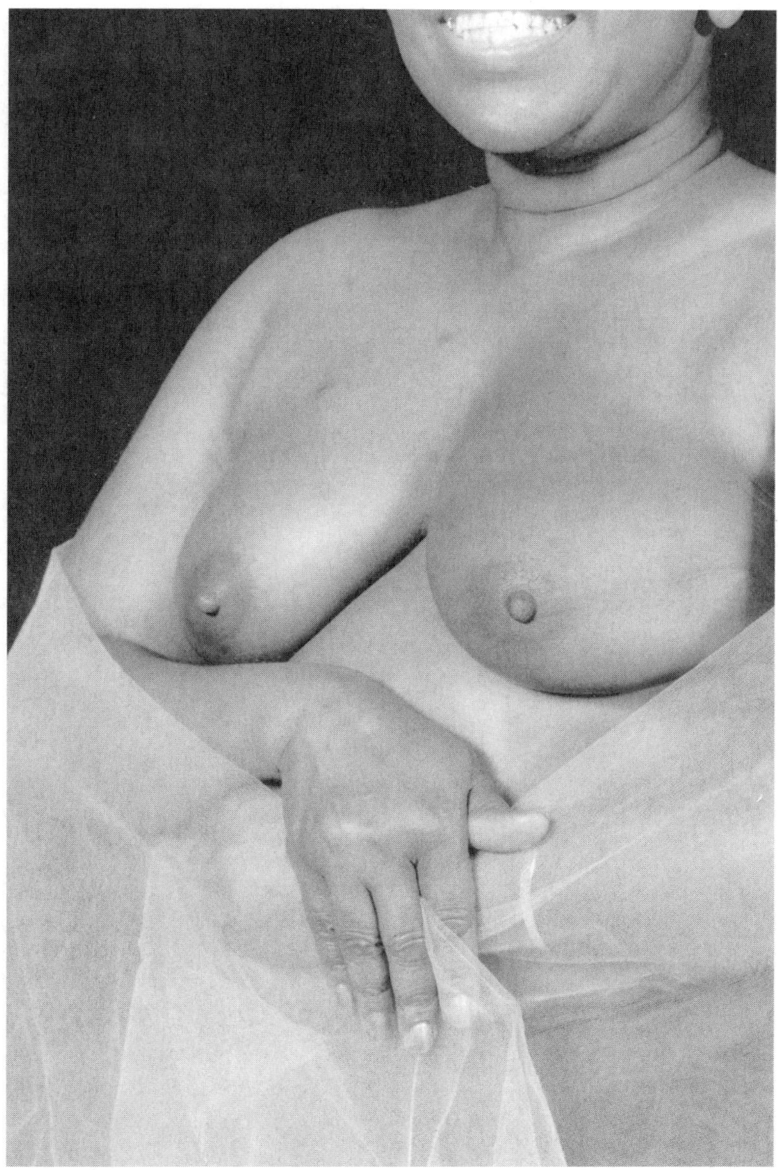

This 50-year-old woman's breast cancer was detected early. She had a lumpectomy, in which the cancerous growth and surrounding tissue were removed.

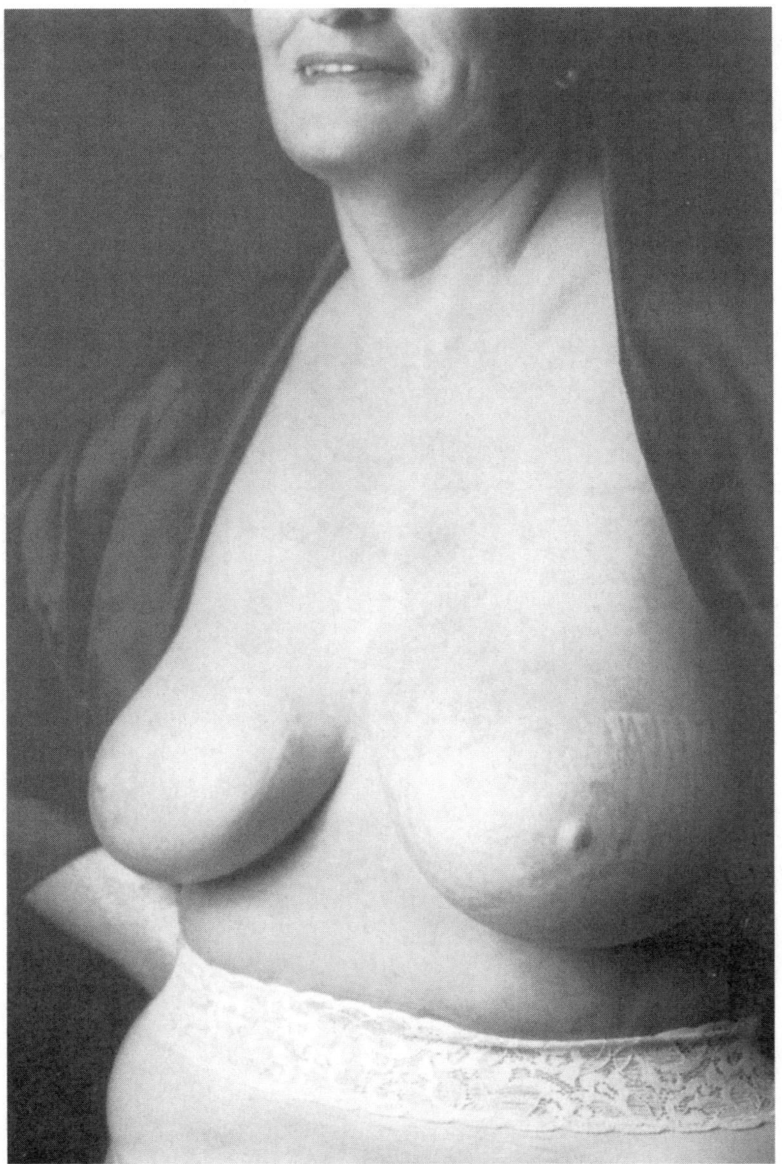

At 47, this woman had both breasts removed. She chose a bilateral (both sides) TRAM flap reconstruction, followed by reconstruction of the nipple and areola.

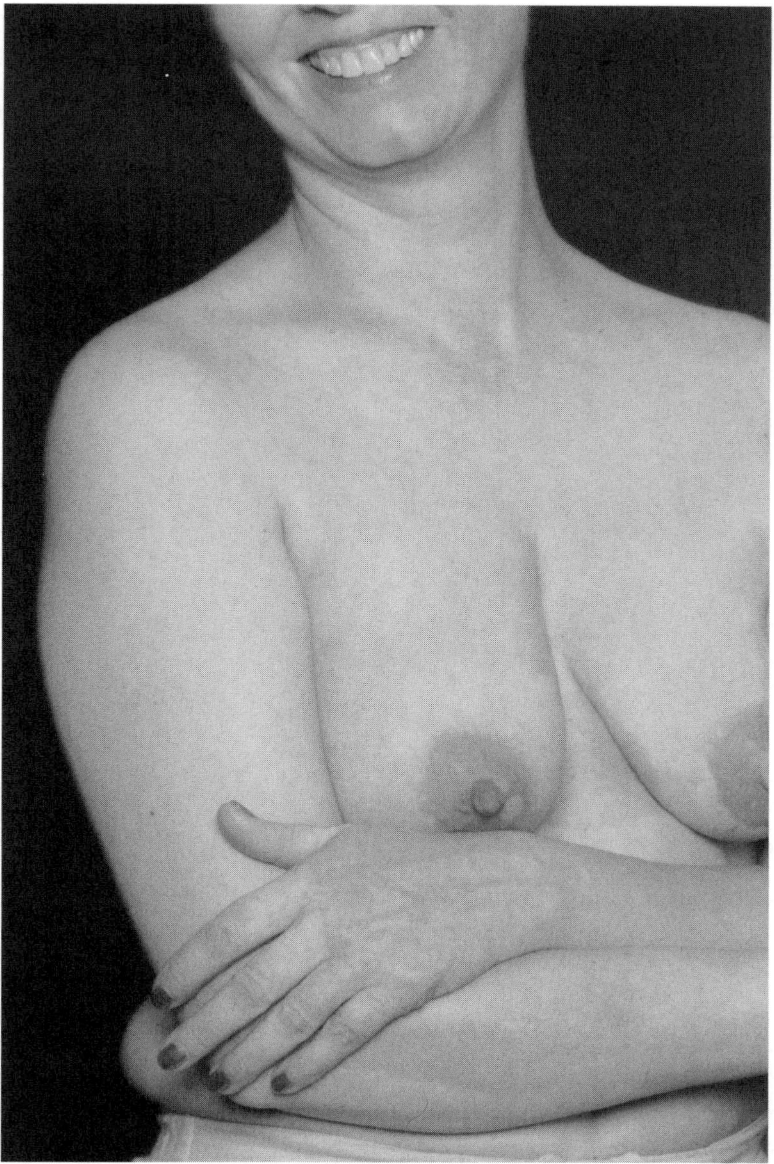

This woman was 43 years old when diagnosed with breast cancer in her left breast. She underwent a lumpectomy, which was followed by radiation therapy. Her scar, on the right side of her left breast, is barely visible.

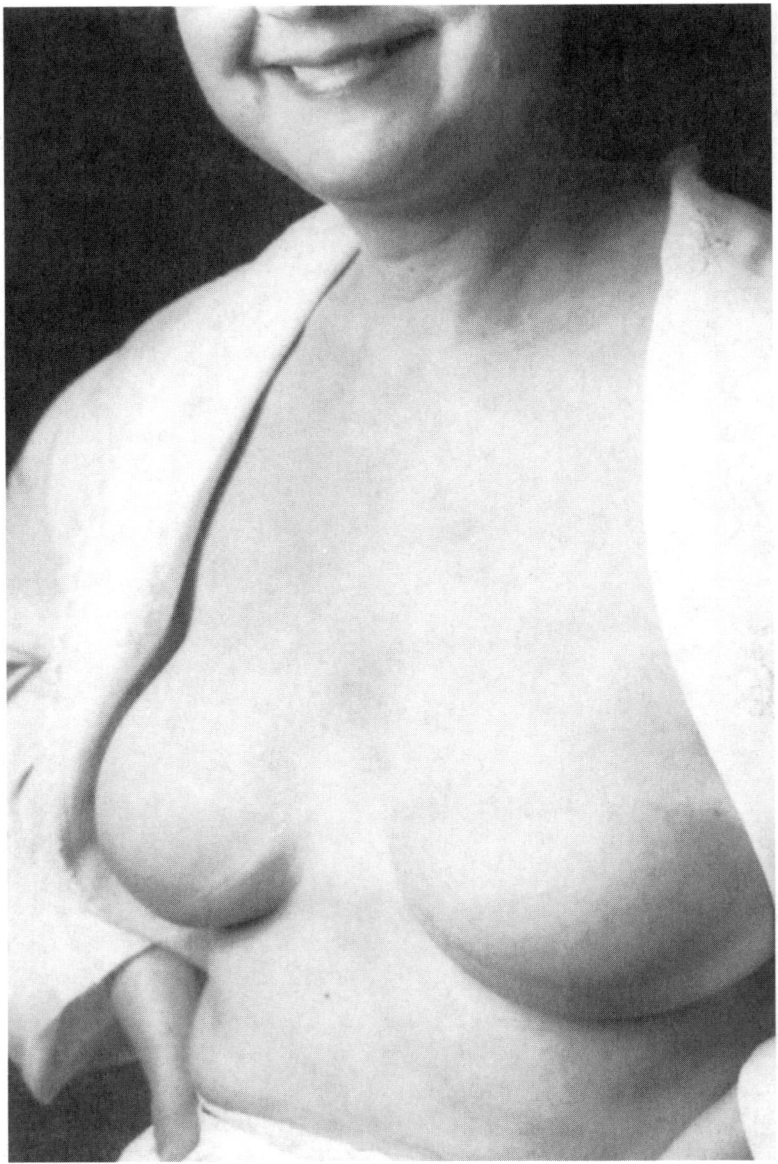

At age 50, this woman had a bilateral mastectomy. She chose to have saline implants and is not planning to have nipple and areola reconstruction.

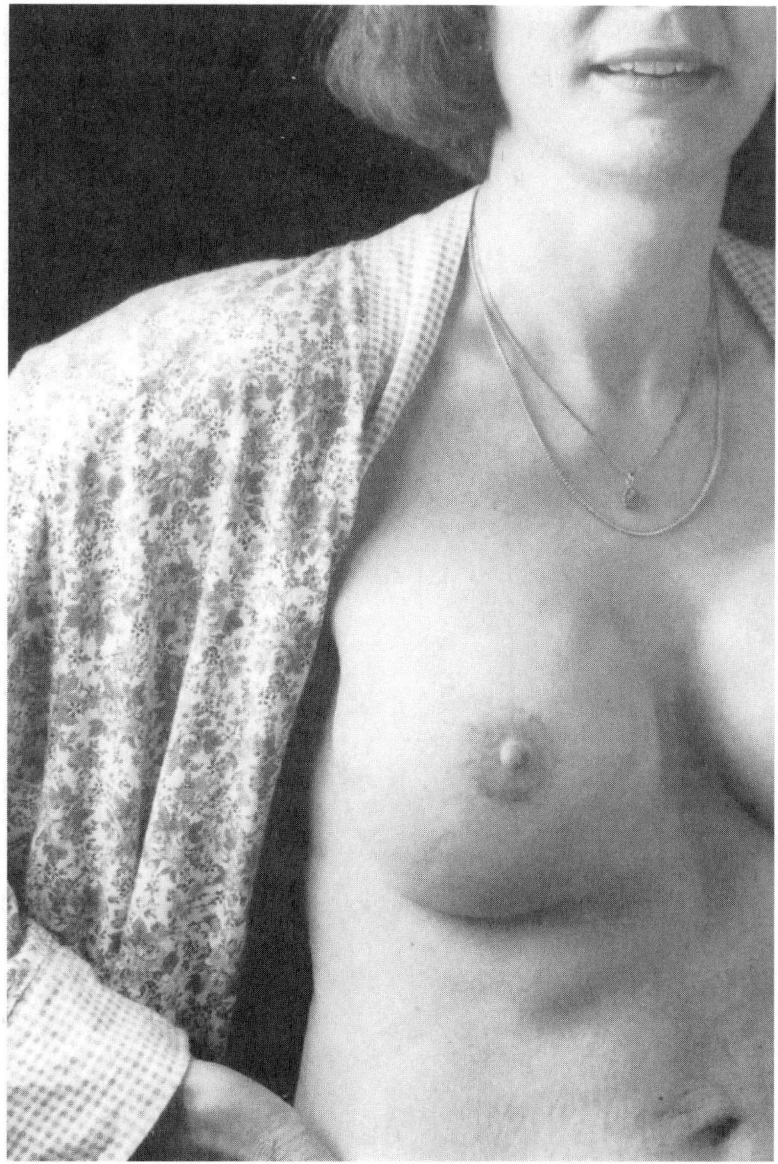

This woman, age 38 at the time of her surgery, chose to have tissue expanders with saline implants. During a second procedure, she had nipple and areola reconstruction.

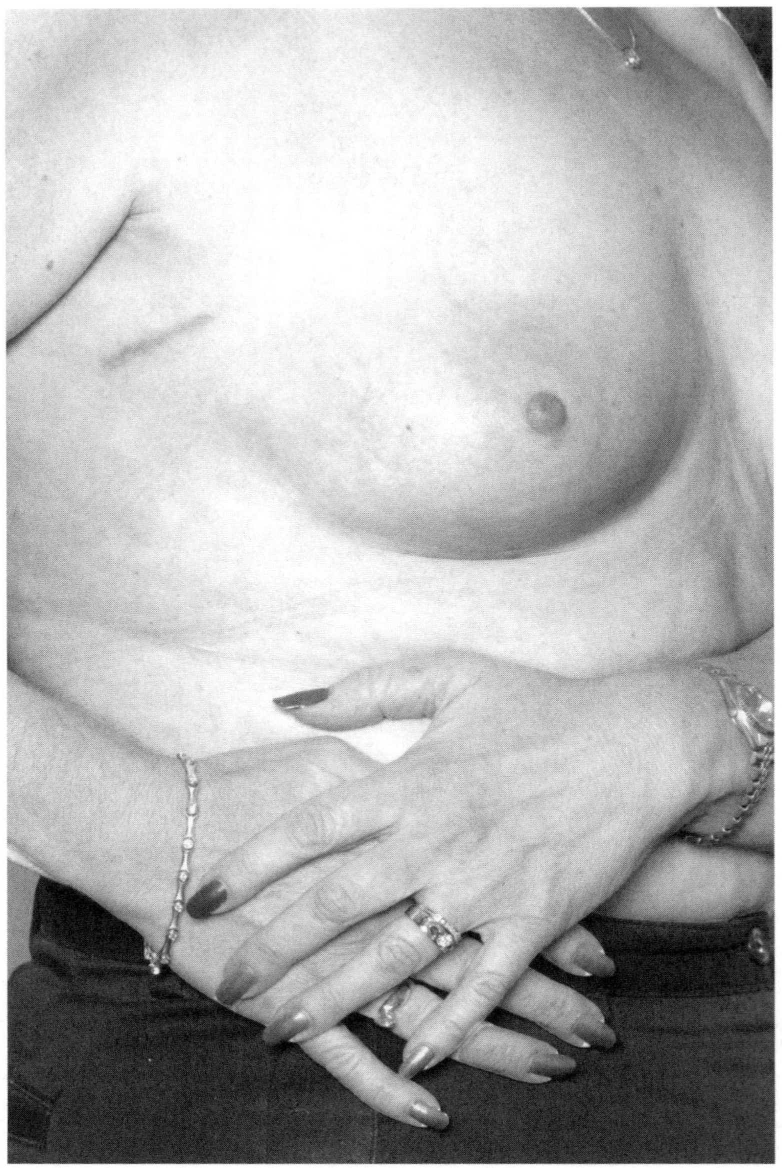

At age 49, this woman chose to have a lumpectomy performed on her right breast. She also underwent six weeks of radiation therapy.

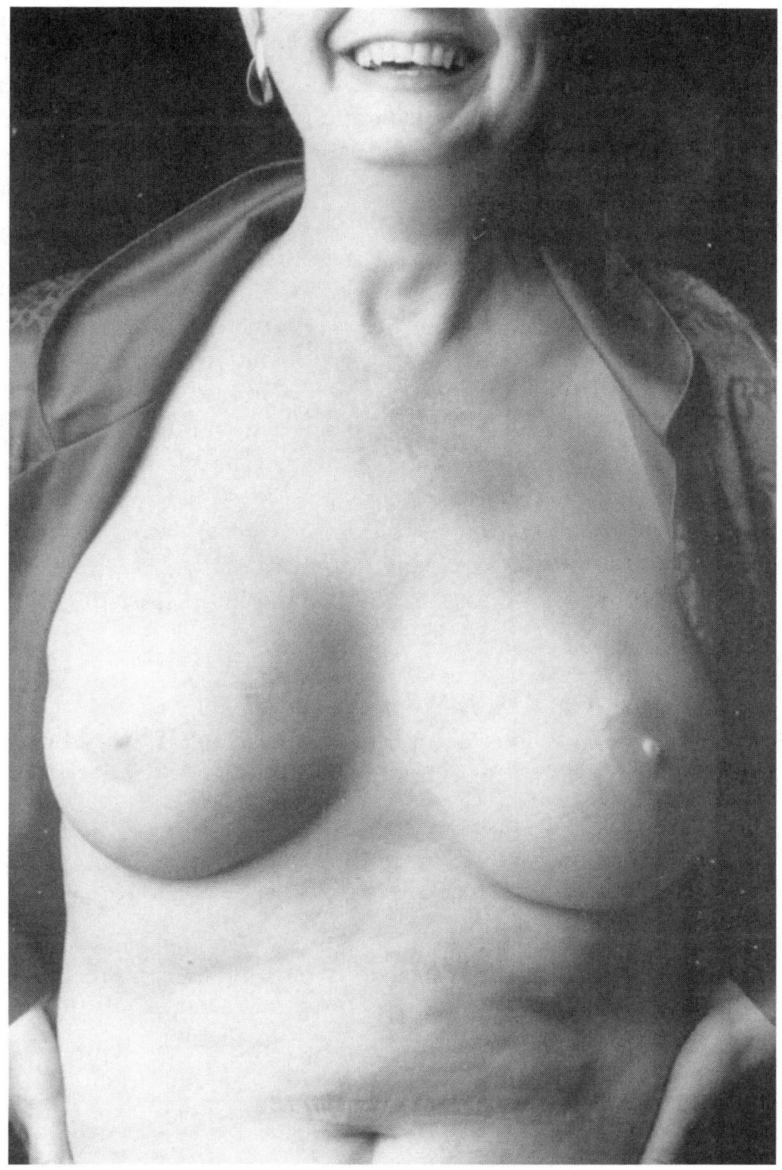

Tissue expanders were inserted immediately following this 46-year-old woman's mastectomy. Saline implants were placed six weeks later, followed by reconstruction of the nipple and areola.

natural than saline implants. Leaks in silicone implants aren't easy to detect, and the gel remains in the body. Controversy about silicone gel led the U.S. Food and Drug Administration in 1992 to issue regulations on silicone-gel breast implants. The FDA didn't ban these implants—no studies have shown that they are harmful—but their use was restricted to women with breast cancer, breast injuries, or breast deformities. However, in 2006, this ban was lifted.

Silicone gel and saline implants come in a variety of shapes and textures. Implants are either round or anatomical, also called teardrop, contoured, or shaped. Round implants typically produce greater fullness on the top of the breast than a natural breast. Anatomical implants are designed to mimic the natural slope of the breast and are fuller at the bottom than at the top. Because of this, anatomical implants are often chosen for reconstruction. An implant's outer shell can be either smooth or textured (similar to fine sandpaper). Round implants come in both varieties. Anatomical implants are available exclusively with textured shells.

Potential Complications with Implants

There are possible complications associated with breast implants. They include the following:

- scar tissue, called a *capsular contracture*, developing around the implant, causing it to be unusually firm
- infection, which may require removal of the implant or the tissue expander
- leakage, which is not hazardous but does require replacement of the implant
- extrusion, in which the skin erodes and the implant shows through. This will require surgery.

Reconstruction with Your Own Tissues

TRAM Flap Reconstruction

Breast reconstruction with your own body tissue often uses skin, fat, and muscle from the lower abdomen—a *transverse rectus abdominis myocutaneous flap*, or *TRAM flap*. In a TRAM flap procedure, blood flow to the transferred tissues is continuous. By contrast, *grafted* tissue is disconnected from its blood supply and quickly moved to its destination elsewhere on the body, where new blood vessels grow into it. Because all body tissues must have a blood supply to survive, any interruption in that supply can endanger the tissues.

Tram Flap

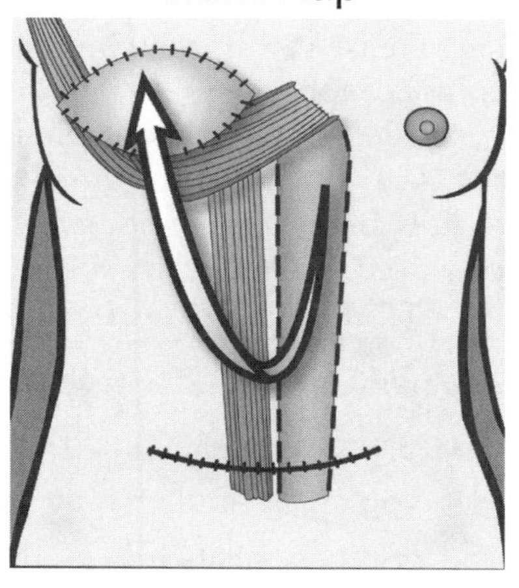

In this procedure, skin, fat, and muscle from the lower abdomen is used. The rectus muscle is disconnected, but left anchored to the rib cage. Then, the skin and fat, which remain attached to the muscle, are rotated upward to form the breast. The fat tissue in the flap helps form the new breast.

During a TRAM flap procedure using abdominal skin, fat and muscle, the surgeon creates a tunnel under the skin through which the tissues will be moved. They remain connected to their blood supply through a muscle that runs from the chest to the pelvis. After the muscle of the abdominal wall has been moved, mesh may be used to reinforce the abdominal wall.

At the chest site, the surgeon shapes the flap to resemble the opposite breast as closely as possible. Because abdominal fat and breast fat are about the same consistency, the new breast usually looks and feels natural. As a bonus, the patient gets a flatter abdomen, since the tissues removed are similar to those removed during a "tummy tuck."

TRAM flap surgery is more extensive than implant surgery, requiring about three to five hours for the procedure, a hospital stay of two to four days, and eight to twelve weeks for full recovery. While you are in the hospital, opioid pain medication is likely to be administered. Your surgeon will probably prescribe opioid pain medication for an additional one to two weeks at home.

If you are a good candidate for this surgery and if your plastic surgeon is well qualified and experienced with TRAM flap breast reconstruction, it is a safe procedure. Although the complication rate is low, there is the potential for infection and complete or partial loss of the transferred tissue. In addition, because the muscle of the abdominal wall has been moved up to the breast, the abdomen may be weakened, resulting in possible hernias.

TRAM flap reconstruction might not be an option for you if:

- you are obese or very thin
- you have abdominal scars from previous surgery
- you are a smoker
- you have diabetes or other blood-vessel disease
- you have lung or heart disease

Free DIEP Flap Reconstruction

A newer variation of the TRAM flap is called a DIEP (Deep Inferior Epigastric Artery) flap. In this procedure, skin and fat are taken from the abdomen and transferred to the breast site. No muscle is transferred, however, which eliminates the need for a mesh on the abdominal wall and lessens the risk of hernias. To create blood flow, tiny blood vessels in the transferred tissue are attached to blood vessels in the breast area. This procedure is technically challenging and requires a surgeon who is skilled in microvascular surgery.

A DIEP procedure takes approximately three to six hours and requires a hospital stay of approximately two to four days. In the hospital, opioid medications are commonly administered, and you can expect to continue taking prescribed opioid medications for one to two weeks. Full recovery takes about eight to twelve weeks. Another variation of this procedure is called the SIEA (Superficial Inferior Epigastric Artery) flap, but it is rarely used.

Latissimus Dorsi Flap Reconstruction

This procedure uses tissues from one of the *latissimus dorsi*—the broad, flat, triangular muscles on the back that are known as "lats." Skin, muscle, and fat are transferred to the front in order to re-create the breast, usually but not always in conjunction with an implant. During the procedure, which takes about two hours, a football-shaped section of skin approximately 8 centimeters wide by 15 centimeters long is tunneled under the armpit to the breast area. An implant or a tissue expander is placed in the same procedure. The main disadvantages of this reconstruction method are a scar on your back and the loss of your lat muscle. Most women, however, function just fine without it.

You can expect to spend about two days in the hospital following this procedure. Opioid pain medications are typically administered in the hospital and are often prescribed for one to two weeks during recovery at home. You can usually drive within about ten days, with full recovery expected at about eight weeks.

Latissimus Dorsi Flap

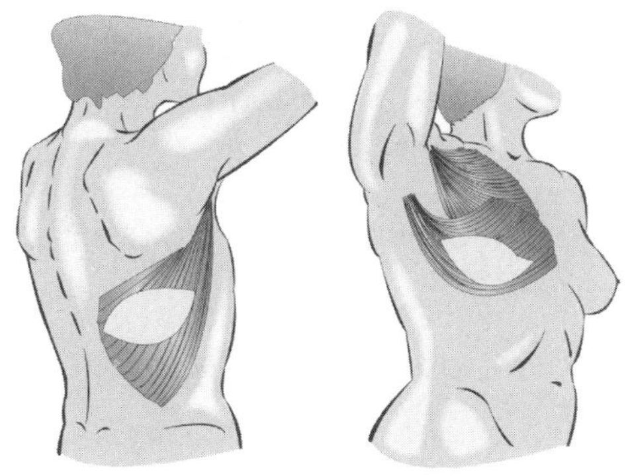

In this procedure, the latissimus dorsi muscle in the back is disconnected, but stays attached at the armpit. The skin and fat, attached to the muscle, are pulled around to form the breast. This procedure usually also requires an implant.

Gluteal Flap Reconstruction

Free flaps taken from the gluteal area are called SGAP (Superior Gluteal Artery Perforator) or IGAP (Inferior Gluteal Artery Perforator). This method uses skin, fat, and muscle from the upper portion of the buttock (SGAP) or lower portion of the buttock (IGAP). In this procedure, a wedge from one of the buttocks is transferred and shaped to form the new breast. The procedure is longer and more complicated than a latissimus flap or TRAM flap. The surgeon must disconnect the blood vessels and then reattach them to the chest wall using an operating microscope. The blood vessels in the buttocks are short and can only be attached to certain vessels that are difficult to reach in the chest area. Because of this, the surgery is technically challenging and not commonly performed.

This procedure is usually not recommended unless you aren't eligible for any other type of reconstruction. With this method, there's a greater risk for tissue loss, and you're left with a scar either on the upper buttock or in the crease below the buttock. Lung deflation during the procedure is another possibility, but is something that can be corrected during the operation.

During implant reconstruction, I was uncomfortable sleeping on my stomach and on my side. I learned to prop up pillows at my back and under my arm to sleep more comfortably.
—Suzanne, 50

The surgery takes approximately four to six hours and requires a hospital stay of about two days. Opioid pain relievers are generally used while in the hospital. At home, you may need to continue taking prescribed opioids for one to two weeks.

Post-Surgical Pain Management

Breast reconstruction is generally associated with more pain than one might experience with lumpectomy or mastectomy, but any discomfort you may feel can be alleviated with medication. The same pain management options used following a mastectomy are used to minimize postoperative pain after breast reconstruction. These options include opioids—which may be administered intravenously, through a "pain pump," with a pain relief ball, or in pill form.

If you're like most women and require a brief hospital stay following breast reconstruction, opioid pain relievers are likely to be administered during this time. Doctors also commonly prescribe opioids for an additional one to two weeks once you return home. You may switch to over-the-counter, nonopioid pain relievers as soon as you feel ready.

Talk to your surgeon prior to your surgery about how your pain will be managed prior to your surgery. It's important to have this matter clarified before you enter the operating room.

Recovery after Breast Reconstruction

In most cases, you can expect your recovery from breast reconstruction to take more time than your recovery from a mastectomy. In general, recovering from breast reconstruction that involves tissues from other areas of the body takes more time than reconstruction using implants. Depending on the type of reconstruction you have, your return to normal activities, such as driving and walking, may take one to two weeks, and in some cases, even longer. Full recovery from breast reconstruction can take as little as five weeks or as much as twelve weeks and depends largely on the type of surgery you choose.

Nipple-Areola Reconstruction

Nipple-areola reconstruction can be performed once you've fully recovered from your implant or flap procedure. The nipple is formed from tissue on the newly reconstructed breast. The areola around the nipple can be recreated by grafting a small piece of skin from elsewhere on the body. This skin graft is usually taken from the abdomen, but can also come from the upper inner thigh or the gluteal crease. After the newly formed nipple and areola have healed, the surgeon can tattoo the areola to make it darker and more natural looking; this can be performed, with a local anesthetic, during an office visit. If you prefer, you can eliminate the areola skin graft and simply have an areola tattooed on the breast mound, but this isn't as natural-looking as a grafted areola.

Nipple-areola reconstruction takes about one hour and is performed on an outpatient basis using anesthesia or a local anesthetic. Recovery time is minimal. Because it contributes to the natural look of the breast, the majority of women who choose breast reconstruction also opt for nipple-areola reconstruction.

Insurance Coverage

Since passage of the 1998 Women's Health and Cancer Rights Act, insurance companies have been required by law to pay for reconstruction of a surgically treated breast and for surgery on the opposite breast if needed. Physical therapy to restore full arm movement after mastectomy, with or without reconstruction, may also be covered by insurance.

Breast Forms or Prostheses

If you decide not to have reconstruction, you can always wear a prosthesis. Many women forgo prostheses as well as reconstruction, for any of a number of reasons: They feel no need to conceal the fact that they've had breast surgery, or they're small-breasted to start with, or they like to wear loose clothing, or they just don't want to be bothered with finding, fitting, and wearing an artificial breast.

It's your call. There are as many ways for a woman to feel and look comfortable and confident as there are women. If you're at your best in tailored, well-fitting clothes, there is no need to sacrifice

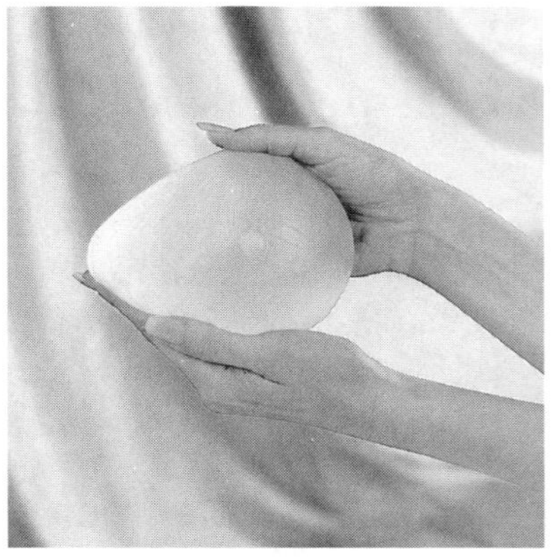

Permanent breast forms are made with silicone gel. *Photo courtesy of Amoena.*

the look you want. Your surgeon or hospital can put you in touch with a volunteer who is knowledgeable about the numerous and attractive styles of breast prostheses. Some are quite economical and look as good as the pricey ones. The cost can vary widely and is often covered by insurance.

Today's breast forms are not only more convenient and comfortable than older ones but can also be matched to your other breast in size, weight, and appearance. Some attach to the chest wall with the help of a small piece of Velcro-like fabric that can remain painlessly in place for several days or weeks. Others can be secured inside a bra. There are special prostheses for swimming or sports, as well as swimsuits and other garments designed for women who have had mastectomies.

You'll find breast prostheses in catalogs, on the Internet, or in specialized lingerie shops, where you can be fitted for one that is precisely the right size and shape for you.

6

Radiation Therapy

Radiation therapy is often prescribed as a follow-up treatment to surgery for breast cancer. Statistics show that radiation therapy can substantially reduce the risk of local recurrence. Cells that are damaged by radiation therapy lose their ability to reproduce, making radiation effective against fast-growing cancer cells. Healthy tissues may also be damaged during treatment; however, the healthy cells heal while the cancer cells do not. Radiation therapy is usually quite tolerable for most women.

Choosing a Radiation Oncologist

A radiation oncologist is a physician who specializes in radiation therapy for cancer patients. Most likely, your surgeon or another physician will refer you to this specialist. The initial consultation is an opportunity for you to discuss treatment benefits and risks with the radiation oncologist, who in all likelihood is someone your referring doctor has worked with many times. You are under no obligation to choose this oncologist, and it is your prerogative to ask for another referral.

Consider having a friend or partner go with you to at least the first meeting with the radiation oncologist—to take notes or ask questions you might forget to ask. Write down as many questions as you can think of in advance. Here are examples of the kinds of things you'll probably be wondering about:

- Will radiation improve my prognosis? To what extent?

- How many treatments will I need? How often will they be given, and for how long?
- Which area will be targeted?
- How much healthy tissue will be exposed to radiation, and where?
- What side effects should I expect, and how can I manage them?

If you live in a rural area or small town, find out where the nearest qualified radiation facility is located. Ask your surgeon or contact the Cancer Information Service of the National Cancer Institute (see the Resources section at the back of this book).

Don't rule out radiation if you live too far from a radiation facility to commute every day. If you don't have friends or relatives who live near a facility and can offer you a place to stay, and you can't afford to stay six weeks or more in a hotel, contact the radiation facility's social worker or patient-support representative. Many medical centers employ people whose job it is to help out with everything from lodging and transportation to financial and family counseling. Programs such as the American Cancer Society's Hope Lodges provide not only free temporary housing during cancer treatment but also a supportive, homelike environment.

When Is Radiation Used?

After Lumpectomy

Radiation therapy after lumpectomy destroys random cancer cells that might remain in the breast or lymph nodes even when the entire tumor, a clean margin, and any of the lymph nodes have been removed. With external beam radiation, the entire breast area is treated by radiation after lumpectomy, including the site from which the tumor was removed.

After Mastectomy

When the entire breast has been removed and no remaining cancer is detected, radiation is usually unnecessary. If the tumor was large, however, or if cancer was found in the margins or in several lymph nodes, radiation is advisable as a safeguard in case surgery did not remove all the cancer cells.

Similarly, if a large amount of cancer has been removed from the inner breast (near the breastbone) or has been found in several underarm nodes, radiation may be used on the lymph nodes behind the breastbone and above the collarbone, since these lymph nodes might also contain cancer cells.

Finally, when a large tumor, five centimeters (two inches) or more, has been shrunk by chemotherapy or hormone-blocking therapy before surgery, radiation after the surgery can reduce the risk of local recurrence.

Delivery of Radiation Therapy

Radiation therapy may be delivered in one of two ways. First, the standard form of radiation therapy involves delivery of radiation externally—called *external beam radiation.* This form of treatment may be used after mastectomy; it can also be used after a lumpectomy.

The second approach, which may be used after a lumpectomy, is referred to as *brachytherapy.* This form or radiation is delivered internally to the lumpectomy cavity through tiny tubes that are inserted into the breast.

Simulation Appointment

If you are to receive external beam radiation, you'll have what's called a simulation appointment with your radiation oncologist and his or her team prior to your first treatment. This is a planning session during which the team will determine the precise area to receive the radiation treatment. This plan will be followed carefully during each treatment.

During the simulation, a customized mold will be made for your arm, back, and neck. This mold will be used during your treatments to hold your upper body in place.

Part of the simulation appointment will also involve the application of some tiny tattoos—black dots about the size of a pinhead—on your chest to indicate the area to be treated. Most women do not find these tattoos to be cosmetically bothersome; however, they can be removed professionally with a laser.

Once the simulation is completed, you'll be scheduled for your first radiation treatment.

External Beam Radiation Therapy

External radiation for cancer treatment reaches its target in the form of a radiation beam, delivered by a machine called a *linear accelerator.* The treatments are painless, much like having an X-ray.

External beam radiation treatments, including preparation, last about ten minutes. A typical treatment schedule is Monday through Friday for three and a half to seven weeks. You're asked to wear no deodorant and no fragrance when you go to the treatment center. Upon arriving, you'll remove your clothes from the waist up and change into a gown. You'll soon become familiar with the treatment routine.

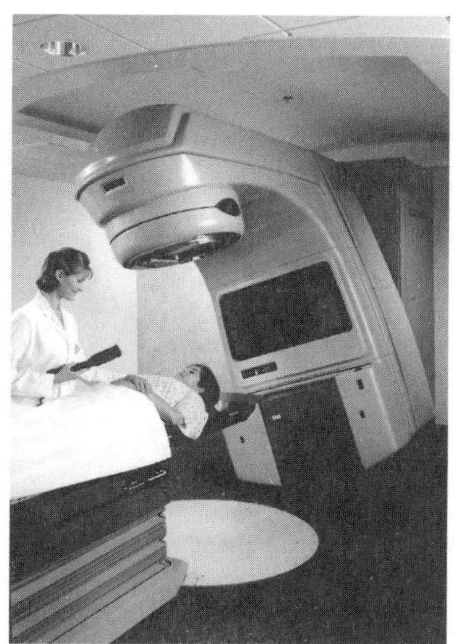

A patient receiving an external-beam radiation treatment. *Photo courtesy of Sieman's Medical Systems, Inc.*

A specially-trained radiation therapist will deliver your treatments. For an external beam radiation treatment, the therapist will usually have you lie on your back; however, some women receive the treatment lying on their abdomen. You'll be asked to lie perfectly still. The radiation machine, which will be above you, will deliver radiation to the tattooed area. The machine will be rotated above you and carefully positioned in two or more places during a treatment session.

Accelerated Breast Radiation Therapy

Some treatment centers are working to shorten the length of time during which whole breast, external beam radiation therapy is given. For example, some doctors are delivering higher doses of radiation over a span of three week instead of the typical period of several weeks. This accelerated approach is called *hypofractionated radiation therapy.*

Boost Treatments

Your initial radiation therapy might be followed immediately by boost treatments that zero in on the site from which the tumor was removed. Whether you receive this "boost" dose of radiation will depend on factors such as age, the size and type of your tumor, the width of the margins, and the size of your breast.

Studies show that boost treatments further reduce the risk of recurrence for all women; however, not every woman will need them. Boost treatments may use external beam therapy, or the radiation may be delivered internally with brachytherapy.

External Boost Treatments

The external boost treatments are similar to the standard external beam treatments; however, the area being treated will be smaller. These boost treatments are usually given daily for one week.

Internal Boost Treatments

The internal boost treatments with brachytherapy may be an option for a woman who has had a lumpectomy. The radiation is delivered to the tumor site from inside the body. Brachytherapy begins with the surgical insertion of multiple, tiny catheters into the area from which the tumor was surgically removed. Then, during a treatment, a radioactive seed is delivered into each catheter.

The brachytherapy may be given at a "high-dose rate" or "low dose rate." The difference between the two doses relates to the time it takes to complete the treatments. The high-dose rate brachytherapy is given on an outpatient basis, twice a day for two to three days; each treatment usually lasts a few minutes. The low-dose brachytherapy is given continuously over a two-day period on an inpatient basis.

Once the treatment is completed, the tiny tubes are removed. If you must travel to a radiation facility for treatment, brachytherapy reduces travel time.

Accelerated Partial Breast Irradiation

A newer form of treatment, *accelerated partial breast irradiation (APBI)*, is becoming an increasingly popular form of radiation treatment for women who have had lumpectomies. APBI can be delivered with external beam radiation or with brachytherapy. It delivers radiation to only part of the breast rather than the whole breast. As a result, the treatment minimizes radiation exposure to healthy tissue, and the treatment takes only about five days rather than several weeks. It can also be delivered prior to chemotherapy. Most women report few side effects.

> ***Radiation was not a bad experience. I actually came to enjoy going every day. In fact, I cried on my last visit because everyone there was so wonderful to me.***
>
> ***—Sandy, 44***

Who is a candidate for partial breast irradiation? Generally, good candidates are women with smaller tumors who have clear surgical margins, have only one site of disease, and have minimal lymph node involvement.

Is APBI effective? Yes it is, according to a 2009 study done at the William Beaumont Hospital in Michigan. This study, which followed up with women ten years after their treatments, showed the same low rate of recurrence (5 percent) among women who received whole breast radiation and those who received partial breast radiation.

Radiation Therapy Side Effects

Because radiation is a localized treatment, it typically has only localized side effects. The majority of women go through radiation treatment with few or minimal side effects. The potential temporary side effects of radiation include:

- swelling of the area
- skin redness, resembling a sunburn
- aches and pains in the treated area (This is not a sign of cancer recurring.)
- fatigue

There is the potential for long-term side effects after radiation therapy. These may include:

- reduced skin elasticity
- a breast that is firmer than normal
- puffiness or change in the size of the treated breast
- change in sensitivity to touch or pressure
- slight darkening or thickening of the skin
- chronic twinges or slight aching in the breast
- arm lymphedema (if lymph nodes received radiation)

Other complications are not likely, but are possible. *Radiation pneumonitis* is a lung reaction that may occur during treatment or weeks to months after treatment; it causes fever, coughing, and shortness of breath. It usually does not require treatment and goes away in a few weeks. It is also possible for radiation therapy to damage the heart; however, modern treatments strive to avoid this. Women who smoke or who have pre-existing heart disease may be more at risk. Finally, women under age 45 have a slight risk (1 in 1,000) for developing cancer five to twenty years later; such cancer may develop in the skin, muscle, bone, or lung.

Radiation therapy for breast cancer will not affect your fertility, menstrual periods, or reproductive system. Some women can breastfeed with the untreated breast and sometimes with the treated breast.

Take especially good care of yourself during your radiation treatment period. These self-care basics can ease your side effects and keep you more comfortable:

- Get plenty of rest.
- Use lukewarm water and mild soap to cleanse the treated area. Do not scrub.
- Wear loose, comfortable clothing during the weeks of treatment. If possible, don't wear a bra.
- Don't use powders, creams, lotions, or deodorants on the treated area before a treatment.
- Ask your radiation oncologist to recommend a cream to use on treated skin after treatments.
- Shield the treated area from sunlight. Some physicians recommend wearing protective clothing or using sunscreen for up to a year following radiation treatment.
- Don't try to scrub or rub off the ink marks—they will fade in time. Tattoos, however, are permanent.

These measures may help keep you comfortable, lift your spirits, manage your side effects, and help you feel more in control during this time of healing.

7

Systemic Therapy

Chemotherapy, Hormone-Blocking Therapy, and Targeted Therapy

After breast cancer surgery, it's possible that some cancer cells still remain in the body. Therefore, *systemic therapy* is recommended to increase long-term survival. This form of treatment uses drugs that travel through the bloodstream to fight cancer. One of the systemic treatments you may be most familiar with is *chemotherapy*, which works to destroy undetected cancer cells that may have spread to areas beyond the location of the original tumor. When chemotherapy follows a primary treatment, such as surgery, the follow-up treatment is called an *adjuvant therapy*.

Another systemic treatment, *hormone-blocking therapy*, works much differently than chemotherapy. Rather than destroy cancer cells, hormone-blocking drugs keep them from reproducing. They do this by depriving cancer cells of the hormones they depend upon.

Yet another form of systemic treatment, *targeted therapy*, involves using drugs to defend against cancer by attaching to specific molecules within or on the surface of cells. As the medical community has learned more about the gene changes in cells that cause cancer, they have been able to develop drugs that target these changes.

Your Medical Oncologist

Adjuvant therapies, such as chemotherapy, are administered by a *medical oncologist*, a physician who specializes in systemic cancer treatments. Your surgeon will refer you to a well-qualified medical oncologist in your area. This physician should be board-certified in medical oncology. To be board-certified, a doctor must have the prescribed training and pass rigorous examinations. This specialist should be someone who inspires your confidence, listens carefully to your questions and concerns, and puts you at ease. You may find it helpful to arrive at each appointment with a list of your questions.

It is important for your doctor to know what medications you are taking, including prescription drugs, vitamins, herbs, and over-the-counter drugs such as aspirin, ibuprofen, sleep aids, and cold medicines.

Chemotherapy

The decision to use chemotherapy depends on such factors as the type of tumor, how aggressive it is, and a patient's age and overall health. Chemotherapy is usually recommended when cancer has spread from the breast to the underarm lymph nodes or when a tumor has aggressive characteristics, whether the nodes are cancerous or not. With smaller tumors and no evidence of cancer in the nodes, chemotherapy is prescribed only on a case-by-case basis.

The term *chemotherapy* refers to a group of drugs, just as the term *antibiotic* refers to many different medications. Chemotherapy drugs act against all rapidly dividing cells—not only cancer cells but also hair cells, gastrointestinal cells, and bone-marrow cells. This explains why hair often falls out during chemotherapy.

The chemotherapy agents listed below each behave differently against cancer cells. Doctors prescribe them in combinations that maximize their benefits. The most commonly used chemotherapy regimens include:

- docetaxel and cyclophosphamide
- adriamycin and cyclophosphamide, which are often followed by docetaxel or paclitaxel (with or without trastuzumab)
- carboplatin, docetaxel, and trastuzumab
- cyclophosphamide with methotrexate and 5-fluorouracil

Other chemotherapy drug combinations may also be utilized; these regimens change frequently as new drugs become available.

Chemotherapy Treatments

There are chemotherapy drugs that you can take at home in pill, capsule, or liquid form. More often, however, chemotherapy drugs are injected or infused (slowly dripped) directly into a vein; occasionally, the chemotherapy is injected into a muscle, under the skin, or into the cancer itself. Only someone thoroughly trained and experienced in the use of chemotherapy can administer drugs in this way, so each treatment requires a visit to the oncologist's office.

Chemotherapy may be given in a vein, or through a small port into the vein that is surgically implanted just under the skin. The port is attached to a tube leading directly to a large vein, and it remains in place until all chemotherapy treatments are finished.

Chemotherapy as Treatment for Breast Cancer

Chemotherapy has been used to treat breast cancer since the late 1960s. However, it was during the 1970s, that its curative powers became known. During this time, chemotherapy was determined to be an effective treatment for women whose breast cancers had spread to nearby lymph nodes. The medical community also learned chemotherapy dramatically decreased a woman's rate of breast cancer recurrence. The increase in the survival rate was striking, and by the 1990s, chemotherapy was recommended for women with stages I through III breast cancer.

The port has numerous advantages. It's usually more convenient for patients since it eliminates the need for repeated needle "sticks." A port is also useful for the delivery of certain medications or when an infusion over several days is needed. It's also useful when conditions such as swelling or obesity make it difficult for medical professionals to find a vein.

If you receive chemotherapy, the dose will be customized especially for you. The goal is to kill as many cancer cells as possible without putting you at undue risk. The range of acceptable dosages is small, but within that range, there is room for differences of opinion. Some oncologists prefer to give the highest acceptable dosages less often; others prefer to give lower dosages more often. As a consequence, your treatments might be weekly, every other week, or even monthly. The nature of each drug and drug combination also determines how often it is given.

Timing of Chemotherapy Cycles

The earlier chemotherapy is given after surgery, the better; there will be fewer cancer cells to attack and the likelihood of success is enhanced. A common chemotherapy regimen begins two to four weeks after surgery and continues for three months to six months.

After surgery and chemotherapy, I also had radiation. I got great support from family and friends. I kept telling myself I would beat this disease.

—Shirley, 58

There is a reason why chemotherapy is given in cycles, or "waves." This approach kills more cancer cells. The first wave of treatment will kill many cells that are just then in the process of dividing. It will miss cells that are at rest, but will kill some of these in the next wave. The cycles of treatment continue with the intent of destroying as many remaining cancer cells as possible. The number and duration of cycles depend on the drugs being used, their dosages, and the stage of the cancer.

Most chemotherapy is given after surgery; however, in some cases, it is better to give the chemotherapy prior to surgery. This approach is called *neoadjuvant chemotherapy.* The intent of this therapy is to shrink a tumor prior to surgical removal. This form of chemotherapy is always recommended for inflammatory breast cancer and often for larger breast cancers; it is especially recommended if a woman is interested in shrinking a tumor so that she can undergo a lumpectomy, which will preserve her breast.

Side Effects of Chemotherapy

Despite the amazing advances in chemotherapy over the years, you'll probably feel a little nervous at first about side effects. It might help to remember that these are only temporary. Side effects vary widely from person to person and drug to drug. Not everyone will have problems with nausea and hair loss. You might be on a different chemotherapy regimen and schedule; you might react differently to the drugs being used; and you might be given different medications to control your side effects.

Low Blood Count

At every treatment, you'll probably have blood drawn and tested. Your doctor will want to make sure that you have adequate levels of red blood cells, white blood cells, and platelets, all of which are essential to your health. All three of these blood components are produced in the *bone marrow*, and when chemotherapy damages bone-marrow cells, the cell-production process slows down. This affects the body in a different way for each component.

Red blood cells carry the oxygen that gives the body fuel for energy, so a reduction in red blood cells causes fatigue and sometimes shortness of breath.

White blood cells fight infection, and when there are fewer white blood cells, the risk of infection increases. If your white blood cell count gets dangerously low, your doctor might briefly postpone your chemotherapy treatment or lower your dosage. Alternatively, he or she might recommend an injection of a growth factor that causes bone marrow to produce and release more white blood cells, enabling you to remain on your normal chemotherapy dosage and schedule. Even so, you will be particularly vulnerable to infection during periods when your cell counts are low, so any signs of infection, such as fever, redness, pain, or swelling, should be promptly reported to your medical oncologist.

When the level of *blood platelets*—cells that aid clotting—becomes low, you may have nosebleeds or bleeding gums, bruise easily, or bleed longer after cutting yourself. If any of these symptoms occurs, notify your doctor right away.

Nausea

Nausea has not been completely eliminated as a side effect of chemotherapy. However, fewer and fewer patients experience nausea during chemotherapy, and those who do can usually manage it well with over-the-counter medicines or prescription drugs, either taken orally or injected. The drugs used most often for nausea are Zofran, Compazine, and Phenergan. If nausea is severe, the drug Emend, taken orally an hour before treatment, is very beneficial. Patients who do experience nausea say it usually lasts a day or two and then subsides.

Eating slowly, and eating small amounts of food at a time—especially dry foods such as toast or crackers—may help, whereas eating heavily right before a treatment is not advised.

> ***I had two rounds of chemotherapy and radiation. But every day puts you in a better place. The greatest lesson I learned was that hard times don't last. You will feel better. Things will get better.***
>
> ***—Ann, 53***

Joint Pain

After chemotherapy, about 5 percent of patients notice short-term or lasting joint pain. Most physicians recommend over-the-counter anti-inflammatory drugs such as ibuprofen. Some doctors say their patients report success in relieving joint pain with chondroitin and glucosamine, nonprescription supplements available at most pharmacies and health-food stores.

Hair Loss

Losing hair is one of the side effects that women find especially emotionally painful. However, the hair not only grows back, but it's not uncommon for the new hair to be thicker, curlier, or even a slightly different color. In some women, the hair only gets thinner rather than falls out completely. Hair loss or thinning can start a few days after chemotherapy begins, but two or three weeks later is more usual.

If you do lose your hair—including eyebrows, lashes, and body hair—it will probably grow back completely within three to five months after you complete chemotherapy. Regrowth sometimes starts even before chemotherapy has ended.

Before your treatment begins, you might want to buy an attractive hairpiece that matches your hair color and is cut and styled the way you like it, or stock up on hats, scarves, and turbans if you find wigs too uncomfortable. Being prepared will help you manage hair loss if it does occur.

A program called "Look Good...Feel Better" puts cancer patients in touch with cosmetologists who provide free advice on makeup and wigs. For more information, see the American Cancer Society listing in the Resources section at the back of this book.

Memory Loss

Some women having chemotherapy report a condition they occasionally refer to as "chemo brain"—a faulty memory that may not improve after the treatments have ended. These women say they are forgetful or "fuzzy-headed" and find it harder to concentrate than they used to, though the condition is almost always mild and doesn't interfere with their ability to hold a job or go about their daily activities.

Study results haven't been unanimous on the cause of this memory loss. Some researchers believe that the problem is a direct result of chemotherapy, most often associated with drugs in the taxane class. Others claim that the memory problems have more to do with hormonal changes, the trauma of being diagnosed with and treated for breast cancer, and sleep disruption.

Fatigue

Women who experience fatigue during the course of their chemotherapy treatments say the first day after treatment is often the most difficult, but the fatigue often lessens in subsequent days. For other women, the onset of fatigue may be delayed. Try to arrange your personal schedule so that you can make time for rest.

Fatigue may increase as the months of chemotherapy progress, and it may persist for a year or two after treatment ends. In cases where fatigue is caused by low blood counts, drugs that stimulate production of red or white blood cells can help. Two such drugs are *epoetin alfa* (Procrit), which is a synthetic form of the human protein *erythropoietin*, and *filgrastim* (Neupogen).

Menopause

Some women stop menstruating during chemotherapy and also may experience the night sweats and hot flashes common in menopause. Other menopausal symptoms include vaginal dryness, fatigue, depression, insomnia, and weight gain.

> ***Breast cancer is like speed bumps in the road. You have rough days or rough procedures, but it gets better. You get over them.***
>
> ***—Kristine, 51***

Younger women usually begin menstruating again after chemotherapy, but women in or near their forties may not. For those who do resume menstruating, fertility is not thought to be affected; they can still conceive and bear children. Remember, temporary cessation of menses during chemotherapy does not necessarily mean you are infertile. So use appropriate birth control measures to prevent pregnancy since chemotherapy drugs can cause birth defects.

Other Side Effects

Other side effects can include mouth sores and taste changes, poor appetite, diarrhea or constipation, tingling or numbness, irritated skin, fluid retention, and brittle nails. Discuss any of these side effects with your doctor, especially if they are persistent or get worse.

Side effects from chemotherapy aren't insignificant, but they need not put your life on hold. Chemotherapy has improved to the point where a majority of working women—60 percent according to one survey—continue working during the course of their treatments. And if you just don't feel up to staying on the job, or you'd rather work part-time on a flexible schedule, discuss your options with your employer.

Hormone-Blocking Therapy

Some types of breast cancer are "fed" by the female hormones—estrogen, progesterone, or both. Hormone-blocking drugs can literally starve these cancers of their needed nutrients. They do this in one of two ways—by interfering with the body's production of estrogen, or by attaching to the hormone receptors of cancer cells. If the drug reaches the receptor first, there's no room for the hormone to attach. With no hormones to feed it, the cancer cell dies.

Hormone-blocking therapy is prescribed when blood tests show that hormone receptors are present, regardless of tumor size or lymph node involvement. One of the advantages of hormone-blocking therapy is that the drugs act against cancer cells without harming normal cells, making these drugs easier to tolerate than chemotherapy drugs.

Hormone-dependent tumor cells have *estrogen receptors* or *progesterone receptors*. Estrogen receptors and methods of blocking estrogen are better understood than progesterone receptors. Even so, women whose tumors have receptors for progesterone but not estrogen appear to benefit from estrogen-blocking therapies.

Hormone-blocking therapy improves a woman's prognosis by reducing the possibility of the same cancer recurring or a new cancer developing. With regular follow-up, the benefits of hormone-blocking therapy are likely to continue at least fifteen years after the five-year treatment period.

Tamoxifen

The drug most commonly used in hormone-blocking therapy is *tamoxifen* (Nolvadex), which belongs to a category of drugs called *selective estrogen receptor modulators* (*SERMs*). These drugs block the effects of estrogen in breast tissue. The first SERM to be developed, tamoxifen was approved for breast cancer treatment by the U.S. Food and Drug Administration in 1978 and remains the only FDA-approved drug for breast cancer prevention. To understand how tamoxifen works, it helps to think of a lock and key. The hormone receptors represent the "lock," and estrogen is the "key" that activates the cancer cells. Tamoxifen fits into the lock but, in effect, doesn't turn the lock; it just gets in the way of the key—the estrogen.

Though tamoxifen has been studied and used since the 1970s, first as a breast cancer treatment and more recently to prevent breast cancer, its precise mechanism isn't well understood. There is evidence that tamoxifen actually becomes incorporated into the cell and directly prevents the next cycle of cell division. The result is not just a temporary block but actual cell death.

> ***I thought if there's a chance it will kill any cancer left in my body, the six-month inconvenience was worth it.***
> ***—Dianna, 33***

To destroy as many cancer cells as possible, tamoxifen is usually given over a five-year period, in a daily dose of 20 milligrams. Tamoxifen therapy usually begins within four weeks after surgery or chemotherapy, or immediately after radiation therapy has ended. Interestingly, while tamoxifen acts against estrogen in cancer cells, it acts very much like estrogen in preserving bone tissue, perhaps offering protection against osteoporosis.

Your doctor will give you a list of drugs to avoid while you're taking tamoxifen. Several drugs, ranging from certain antidepressants to anti-allergy medications, can affect the effectiveness of tamoxifen.

Other Hormone-Blocking Drugs

Other SERMs have been developed and continue to emerge as scientists attempt to replicate the benefits of tamoxifen without the side effects. *Raloxifene* (Evista), which is a drug approved for osteoporosis prevention, has been shown by studies to be as effective as tamoxifen in preventing breast cancer in high-risk postmenopausal women. Raloxifene carries a very slight risk of strokes that, although extremely rare, are more likely to be fatal.

Goserelin (Zoladex) is probably better known as a prostate-cancer drug. Just as it suppresses testosterone production in men, it suppresses estrogen production in premenopausal women, bringing on temporary menopause, with menopausal symptoms being the only side effects.

Aromatase inhibitors—anastrozole (Arimidex), *letrozole* (Femara), and *exemestane* (Aromasin)—block estrogen production in postmenopausal women by inhibiting the enzyme *aromatase.* This enzyme converts other hormones to estrogen and is the body's principal source of estrogen after menopause. Arimidex is used either as a first hormone-blocking treatment or when other drugs, such as tamoxifen, have not fully halted the disease. Its side effects can include fatigue, hot flashes, nausea, back pain, bone pain, decreased bone density, some hair loss, and blood clots. Femara and Aromasin, also effective against tumors that resist tamoxifen, have milder side effects.

Side Effects of Hormone-Blocking Drugs

Your doctor will give you a list of possible side effects of hormone-blocking drugs; they include vaginal dryness, fatigue, depression, hot flashes, weight gain, insomnia, and memory loss.

Tamoxifen has been linked to a slightly higher risk of uterine cancer. You should not take tamoxifen if you have a history of blood clots. Years ago, when tamoxifen was prescribed in much higher doses, women taking the drug occasionally suffered eye damage. This side effect is extremely rare with today's lower doses, but you should still have regular eye exams while you are on tamoxifen.

Targeted Therapy

The term *targeted therapy* refers to the use of bio-engineered drugs that interfere with cancer-causing mechanisms at the molecular level. Some targeted-therapy drugs represent truly astonishing accomplishments in genetic engineering. Side effects are typically mild because healthy cells aren't damaged.

Targeted-Therapy Drugs

The best-known drug used in targeted breast cancer therapy is *trastuzumab* (Herceptin). Approved by the FDA in 2006, Herceptin works on the surface of the cancer cell by blocking the chemical signals that can stimulate uncontrolled growth. However, the drug is recommended only for those women whose breast cancer tumors are HER2/neu-positive.

I didn't want to go through chemo; I didn't want to lose my hair, but I did. Later, at stop signs, I used to whip off my wig on the hot drives home from work and enjoy the astonishment on the faces of other drivers.

—Suzanne, 58

Herceptin is neither a hormonal therapy drug nor a chemotherapy drug. Rather, it is a *monoclonal antibody*—biologically engineered to act against the HER2/neu protein expressed by the HER2 gene. As described in chapter 2, HER2/neu "overexpression" is a factor in 20 to 30 percent of breast cancers, occurring when women have more than the normal pair of HER2 genes. These types of tumors tend to grow and spread more quickly than tumors that are not HER2/neu-positive.

Herceptin is given intravenously in a doctor's office. Infusions will usually last from thirty to ninety minutes, depending on your dosage, the frequency of your infusions, and how well you tolerate the infusions. The drug is added to a chemotherapy regimen and continues after the chemotherapy, for a total of one year.

Even though Herceptin may cause mild side effects, it does not cause hair loss or nausea, often associated with chemotherapy. In about 40 percent of women, the drug may cause flu-like symptoms such as fever, chills, nausea, or muscle aches; these symptoms usually diminish after the initial treatment. In rare cases, Herceptin may cause heart failure. In these cases, the drug can be stopped and the patient may regain full heart function with the help of heart-strengthening medications.

A newer drug called *lapatinib* (Tykerb) is used in targeted breast cancer therapy. Tykerb, which blocks the HER1 and the HER2 genes, is in the class of drugs called *tyrosine kinase inhibitors.* In simple terms, Tykerb blocks protein expression inside the cancer cell while Herceptin acts on protein on the cell's surface.

Is Systemic Therapy Right for You?

> ***Chemotherapy was relatively easy for me. I followed directions, and my family was considerate of my lack of energy. I bought a wig the same color as my hair and, for the most part, continued on with my life.***
> ***—Carolyn, 65***

If you have not begun menopause, your doctor is more likely to prescribe chemotherapy than hormone-blocking therapy. For one thing, tumors in premenopausal women tend to lack hormone receptors—they are not dependent on hormones in order to grow. In addition, younger women tend to have faster-growing tumors than older women, and they have more years ahead of them in which cancer could recur. Chemotherapy can effectively reduce this long-term risk.

The reverse is true after menopause. Because their tumors are often slow-growing and hormone-dependent, postmenopausal women are more likely to receive hormone-blocking therapy.

Both therapies are given when conditions call for them. For example, a woman with a hormone-dependent cancer that has spread to the lymph nodes or is larger than one centimeter is likely to receive chemotherapy followed by hormone-blocking therapy, whether she is premenopausal or postmenopausal.

Research Continues

Scientists are eagerly pursuing targeted therapies using many different mechanisms to combat cancer. Some work by replacing missing or defective genes with "good" copies of the gene, sometimes using viruses as transportation. Other experimental targeted therapies use stem cells to deliver anticancer agents directly to tumor metastases, or vaccines to find and destroy cancer-promoting proteins.

As more is learned about genetic cancer triggers, more therapies will be developed to address these abnormalities. Treatments that were unimaginable twenty years ago are saving lives today. The potential for future breakthroughs is truly exciting.

8

If Cancer Recurs

If your breast cancer has responded well to therapy, you have every reason to celebrate—treatments have worked, you have survived, and your life can return to normal. However, if you are like most women, somewhere in the back of your mind you fear that the cancer will recur or that a new cancer will develop in your other breast. You may also worry that your breast cancer has put your daughter, sister, mother, or granddaughter at higher risk.

Some women first confront these kinds of fears when the initial shock of diagnosis wears off and surgery is over. Others don't begin worrying until they have finished radiation therapy or adjuvant therapy. When you stop making frequent visits to familiar doctors and nurses, you may feel strangely vulnerable. For example, you may feel a wave of anxiety with every small headache or bodily pain, certain that the cancer is back.

Fortunately, the intense anxieties subside with time. Most women begin relaxing a little after each checkup until two years, and then five, have finally passed. Although breast cancer has been known to recur as late as twenty-five years after the first diagnosis, it is most likely to reappear within the first five years, and especially the first two. After the ten-year mark, a woman's risk of recurrence is very small.

Risk of Recurrence

Keep in mind that 70 to 90 percent of the women diagnosed with early-stage breast cancer never have a recurrence after treatment. Well over half of the women who experience a recurrence live ten years or more after treatment for the recurrence. Here again, early detection is key: The sooner a new tumor is discovered, the better the chances for recovery. Finally, there's a great deal you can do to keep your body strong and less vulnerable to recurrence.

In chapter 1, we discussed the general risks linked to primary breast cancer—the various environmental, hereditary, and behavioral factors thought to play a role in the development of this disease. To understand your risk of recurrence, consider these factors as well as the ones associated with your particular kind of breast cancer.

The same cancer characteristics that were used to guide your treatments will also help to estimate your risk of recurrence. These characteristics include:

- tumor size
- lymph-node involvement
- presence or absence of hormone receptors
- rate of cancer-cell division (Poorly differentiated cells divide rapidly, well-differentiated cells divide less often.)
- cell DNA content (Diploid cells have normal amounts of DNA; aneuploid cells have abnormal amounts of DNA.)
- percentage of cells dividing in the tumor at any given time (the S-phase fraction)
- presence of micrometastases
- HER2/neu overexpression
- BRCA1 or BRCA2 gene mutation
- Ki-67 and p53 tumor markers

Breast cancer can reappear at the site of the original tumor as a *local recurrence* or in another part of the body as a *distant recurrence,* or *metastasis.* Though it can spread to many different locations, the most common breast cancer metastases affect the lymph nodes, liver, lungs, and bones. After the lymph nodes, the bones are the most likely site for metastasis, apparently offering breast-cancer cells a hospitable tissue and blood supply where they can multiply and thrive.

Ask your doctor about your specific risk of recurrence, realizing that, no matter how scientifically your risk factors and cancer characteristics are combined and analyzed, the outlook is only an indication, not a prediction. Cancer, by definition, is unpredictable, and most kinds of cancer cells have both "good" and "bad" traits, so it's impossible to be certain how a cancer will behave. Living each day with hope and a positive attitude can go a long way toward redeeming a less-than-positive prognosis.

One of the best strategies for long-term survival is to pay close attention to your body—using common sense, of course, so that you're not in a continual fret. Using the information in this book and other sources, you've learned the signs and symptoms of breast cancer. Now, become equally familiar with the warning signs of breast cancer recurrence. The better you understand the genuine warning signs, the more relaxed you'll probably be about unrelated symptoms.

Let your doctor know at once if you experience:

- bone pain
- headaches
- muscle weakness or numbness
- shortness of breath
- persistent cough
- weight loss or lack of appetite

Risk of a New Cancer

It is only fair to think that if you have had breast cancer once, you should not have to worry about it twice. But cancer is never fair, and sometimes a new primary cancer does develop, in a breast treated with lumpectomy, in the untreated breast, or, less commonly, in a small amount of breast tissue left behind after mastectomy. Fortunately, the risk of a second breast cancer remains small—about 0.5 to 1 percent per year after your first diagnosis. If you have had a very aggressive cancer, you may be more likely to develop breast cancer again.

There are some women who have an inherited tendency to develop a series of primary cancers. Those who have this unusual condition might recover from breast cancer only to face other cancers in other parts of the body. For information, talk with your doctor, or call the Hereditary Cancer Institute (see the Resource section).

Follow-Up Care and Prevention

Physicians today have several strategies for reducing your risk of further cancer, and new strategies are being studied all the time. It is vitally important to continue getting the care you need, after your successful cancer treatment, to help catch any recurrence at its earliest stage. The danger of random, microscopic cancer cells remains, and if such cells find the right place to grow, they can form a new tumor.

I always wonder if the cancer will return. I don't always talk about it, but the scare is there at times. One day at a time...that's how you live with cancer.

—Liz, 42

Your follow-up care will be more frequent and comprehensive during the first year or so after your surgery. Depending on the treatment you received, you'll visit your cancer surgeon, radiation oncologist, medical oncologist, and plastic surgeon (if you have had reconstruction). Your primary physician, the one who has coordinated your care throughout your treatment, will probably be involved in your follow-up care as well. He or she should be in touch with all the members of your medical team throughout the follow-up period, and you'll probably see this doctor every six months or so for a complete physical examination. Your primary physician or other doctors may also order diagnostic tests as part of your follow-up care.

Blood Tests

After you have had systemic therapy, you'll probably have monthly blood tests until your blood counts stabilize. Your doctor might also use blood tests that look for *tumor markers,* abnormally high amounts of substances, such as certain kinds of proteins, that might indicate when a tumor is present. The tests are not sensitive enough to find a recurrence at its earliest stages, since a tumor must be large enough to release detectable amounts of the marker substances. Results sometimes include false-negatives. Thus, the most appropriate use of these tests is in following a known recurrence to gauge its response to therapy.

Other blood tests look for elevated levels of enzymes that sometimes indicate the presence of cancer in the liver or bone. If test results suggest a problem with the liver, you may have a PET/CT scan to investigate further. If tests show that bone cancer could be present, or if you experience bone pain, your doctor will order a bone scan.

Preventing Cancer Recurrence

- Engage in three or more hours of moderate exercise each week.
- Eat a balanced, healthful diet.
- Control weight.
- Avoid alcohol.
- Control blood sugar, if diabetic.

Scans

The first step in a *bone scan* is injection of a harmless radioactive liquid into the bloodstream. After a few hours, the radioactive particles are taken up by the bones, where they concentrate in areas of increased blood circulation that could indicate cancer. Such areas, called "hot spots," are detected by a machine that scans your body from above while you are lying on a table. Hot spots can appear for many reasons—injury, arthritis, or other problems besides rapidly dividing cancer cells—and the machine cannot distinguish the cause. Therefore, if a bone scan finds an area of increased circulation, it will be followed up by an X-ray, PET/CT scan, or MRI, which can show more clearly what is going on at that site.

PET/CT Scan. A PET/CT scan combines these two types of tests, each yielding different information. Equipment is now in use that performs both scans at the same time. More often, the scans are done separately and the results are compiled into one report.

A *Computerized Tomography (CT)* uses radiation to display cross sections of the body, which can reveal cancers deep within the body or brain. During the scan, you'll need to lie very still while the CT machine takes X-ray pictures from many different angles. A computer assembles these slices of images into a detailed picture of the scanned area. In a *spiral* or *helical CT scan,* the X-ray beam rotates around you in a spiral. It is faster than a standard CT scan and may find smaller tumors.

A *Positron Emission Tomography (PET) scan* detects chemical changes not apparent with a CT scan alone. The procedure is painless but can be tedious. After receiving an injection of a radioactively labeled sugar, which cancer cells absorb more fully than normal cells, you'll have to lie still for up to two hours—first while the sugar is absorbed and then as the table you're lying on moves through the scanner.

> ***I chose a double mastectomy because I didn't want to have to worry about recurrence. I am glad I made the decision.***
>
> ***—Billie, 48***

Magnetic Resonance Imaging (MRI). An MRI uses magnets instead of X-rays to take many pictures from a variety of angles. The MRI can find soft-tissue abnormalities that other tests may overlook.

Liver Scan. Your doctor may order a CT scan or ultrasound of your liver to see if cancer is present there.

Chest X-Rays

Breast-cancer survivors are usually advised to have a chest X-ray every year, or at any time if you experience shortness of breath or develop a persistent cough.

Breast Self-Examination and Mammography

Of course, self-examination and mammograms remain critical after cancer treatment. If you have had a lumpectomy, you should examine both breasts and the entire breast area, as outlined in chapter 2. If you have had a mastectomy, you should examine your untreated breast, the surgical site, and the surrounding area, paying attention to your incision and chest wall for thickness, lumps, or rigidity. Report any suspicious changes to your doctor immediately.

Most experts recommend a mammogram about six months after treatment. If you have had a lumpectomy, a mammogram of the surgically treated breast will serve as a new baseline. The other breast will look about the same on the new image as on earlier ones. If you have had a mastectomy, a physical examination of your incision, armpit, breast area, and the area above your collarbone will be sufficient—but, of course, you should have routine mammograms done on your opposite breast. Most physicians recommend mammograms every six months for the first year or two after cancer treatment, and then annually after that.

Tamoxifen

If your original tumor tested positive for hormone receptors, you have probably begun a five-year course of hormone-blocking therapy, most likely with tamoxifen, which kills cancer cells by keeping them from dividing. Tamoxifen has not only been shown to prevent primary breast cancer in some high-risk women but also to keep it from recurring in women who have already had breast cancer. The drug also shrinks existing tumors and is used against breast-cancer metastases. Like all anti-cancer drugs, it has risks and side effects as well as benefits, so you should ask your doctor to discuss these with you.

Pamidronate (Aredia)

A class of drugs called *bisphosphonates* disrupt the normal cycles in which bone breaks down and regenerates to keep the skeletal system healthy. *Pamidronate* (Aredia) is the most commonly prescribed bisphosphonate for this use. If your doctor thinks it would be beneficial in your case, you'll probably receive an injection of pamidronate every few weeks.

Treatment for Recurrence

The return of breast cancer to the original site or elsewhere in the body is called a recurrence. (If the reappearance of cancer actually represents cancer cells from the original tumor that weren't removed during treatment, then it's technically not a recurrence, though the remainder of this chapter will use the word "recurrence" to refer to newly active breast cancer from whatever cause.)

Local Recurrence

Cancer that reappears after lumpectomy, at the site of the original tumor, is one form of local recurrence. Radiation isn't an option for treating the cancer, since you will have had radiation after your lumpectomy, and repeated radiation would cause too much tissue damage. Your doctor will probably want to perform a mastectomy as the best way of removing all the cancer.

> ***You have to be an advocate for your own health. If you notice a change in your breast or a change in how you are feeling, get checked. We'd much rather have a false alarm than miss something important.***
>
> ***—Stephen, medical oncologist***

Local recurrence after mastectomy can appear in the surgical scar, in the skin or fat where the breast was, in the muscle or bone of the chest wall, or in a remnant of breast tissue left behind after the surgery. Surgery is the first line of treatment, to remove the cancer and any affected tissue, muscle, or bone. If you didn't have radiation to the site after your mastectomy, radiation can now be used on the entire breast area to eradicate any microscopic traces of the cancer.

Most cases of local recurrence are treated locally, with surgery and in some cases radiation. If the original tumor tested positive for hormone receptors, the woman will already be on a five-year regimen of tamoxifen or another hormone blocker. But if there is a chance that the local recurrence signals a wider metastasis, chemotherapy will be prescribed as well. For example, if the recurrence is in the mastectomy scar, the cancer has probably traveled there through the bloodstream and lymph nodes. The danger, of course, is that it has traveled elsewhere in the body as well. In this case, chemotherapy may halt any microscopic spread of the disease.

New chemotherapy drugs, in new combinations and dosages, are being tested and introduced all the time. Some of these are especially promising against recurrent cancer. The more your doctor stays informed about such developments, and aware of the conditions under which each drug or combination is most useful, the better he or she will be able to fine-tune your treatment and maximize its results.

Metastasis, or Distant Recurrence

When breast cancer has spread to another part of the body, treatment must be as aggressive as possible, while keeping side effects tolerable. The same therapies are available for metastases as for a primary cancer—surgery, radiation (in areas not previously irradiated), and systemic therapies—though they may be used differently, and in different combinations or sequences, than with a primary cancer. Radiation is sometimes successful both in relieving the pain of metastases and in destroying the new tumor. In other cases, if a new tumor is localized and readily accessible to surgery, the recurrent cancer can be removed. Adjuvant therapies are used to decrease the incidence of inevitable metastatic disease.

Different systemic drugs may be used in different combinations for breast-cancer metastases than for primary breast cancer. The focus among researchers is to develop new treatments that are at least as effective as ones currently in use, but with milder side effects and fewer risks.

Quality of Life

Whether your cancer recurs or you worry that it will, there are any number of things you can do to boost your confidence, protect your well-being, and feel in control over important aspects of your life. Many breast-cancer survivors suggest living one day at a time, paying attention to the things that matter most—eating well, exercising, meditating, pursuing a spiritual search, finding creative expression, nurturing the relationships that sustain you—doing the things that fuel your energy and give you the greatest satisfaction. Try to reestablish routines and challenges that were interrupted by your illness. Add new ones, ways of reaching out and enriching your life.

As mentioned in chapter 3, a support group can offer priceless help and new friendships. Consider working with organizations that promote breast-cancer awareness and research. You might work with survivors like yourself or with women just recently diagnosed, who need to see what you represent—life going on. Activism has been responsible for many strides against breast cancer in recent years. You could make a difference by battling this disease on a new front, in small or energetic ways. There is always something you can do. Your life remains your own.

> ***When my cancer recurred, I was really angry. I told my sister, 'I can't do it.' But she convinced me that I did it once and I could do it again.***
>
> *—Jean, 48*

In Good Company

(an inner dialogue)

"What do you mean, it was cancer?"
(I am too busy for that.)

"Yes, I'll be there in the morning"
(I don't mind losing a breast.)

"Please turn the morphine pump higher"
(Oh my God, this really hurts.)

"Your chemo will last only six months"
(Oh, well, a baby takes nine.)

"Is that a wig? You look stunning!"
(Surely he's flattering me.)

"Welcome: Breast Cancer Support Group"
(I am in good company.)

—Suzanne W. Braddock, M.D.

Resources

AMC Cancer Research Center & Foundation

1600 Pierce Street
Denver, CO 80214
Phone: (303) 233-6501 or (800) 321-1557(800) 535-3777
Cancer Information and Counseling Line
www.amc.org

AMC Cancer Research Center is a not-for-profit research institute dedicated to the prevention of cancer and other chronic diseases. American Medical Center became the first institution in the country to devote its scientific resources entirely to the prevention of cancer. AMC is conducting cancer research in the areas of causation and prevention, nutrition in the prevention of disease, health communications, behavioral research, and community studies.

American Cancer Society (ACS)

15999 Clifton Road NE
Atlanta, GA 30329-4251
Phone: (800) ACS-2345 or (800) 227-2345
www.cancer.org

With more than two million volunteers and 3,400 local units, the ACS works to eliminate cancer as a major health problem through prevention, saving lives, and diminishing suffering through research, education, patient services, advocacy, and rehabilitation.

The ACS also sponsors the "Look Good. Feel Better," a free, non-medical, brand-neutral, national public service program created to help individuals with cancer look good, improve their self-esteem, and manage their treatment and recovery with greater confidence. Visit www.lookgoodfeelbetter.org.

American Cancer Society also sponsors the Hope Lodge in many cities; each Hope Lodge offers cancer patients and their families a free, temporary place to stay when their best hope for effective treatment may be in another city. For more information, visit ACS.org and enter "Hope Lodge" in the search box.

Avon Breast Cancer Crusade
Avon Foundation Breast Care Fund

Coordinating Center
505 Eighth Avenue, Suite 1601
New York, N.Y. 10018
Phone: (212) 244-5368
www.avoncrusade.com
www.avonbreastcare.org

An initiative of Avon Products, Inc. that began in 1993, the mission of the Avon Breast Cancer Crusade is to fund access to care and finding a cure for breast cancer. The organization puts a particular focus on medically under-served populations.

Bone Marrow Transplant InfoNet

2900 Skokie Valley Road, Suite 104
Highland Park, IL 60035
Phone: (847) 433-3313 or (888) 597-7674
Fax: (847) 433-4599
www.bmtnews.org

The Blood and Bone Marrow Transplant InfoNet is a non-profit organization that provides information to bone marrow, peripheral blood stem cell, and cord blood transplant patients.

Breast Cancer Network of Strength

(Formerly Y-Me National Breast Cancer Organization)
212 W. Van Buren, Suite 500
Chicago, IL 60607
Phone: (312) 986-8338
Fax: (312) 294-8597
24-hour Breast Cancer Network of Strength Hotlines:
(800) 221-2141 English(800) 986-9505 Spanish
www.networkofstrength.org

The mission of the Breast Cancer Network of Strength is to decrease the impact of breast cancer, increase breast cancer awareness, and to ensure through information, empowerment, and peer support, that no woman faces breast cancer alone. Founded in 1978, the organization has matured from a kitchen table support group of 12 women to a national organization with affiliate partners in 27 cities throughout the United States. The site is available in both English and Spanish versions. A 24-hour-a-day hotline is offered.

Cancer Care, Inc.

275 7th Avenue, 22nd Floor
New York, NY 10001
Phone: (800) 813-HOPE or (212) 712-8400
www.cancercare.org

A nonprofit organization since 1994, Cancer Care offers emotional support, information, and practical help to people with all types of cancer and their loved ones. All services are free. Forty-five oncology social workers are available for phone consultations in which they provide emotional counseling and support; Cancer Care also offers education seminars, teleconferences, and referrals to other services.

Celebrating Life Foundation

P.O. Box 224076
Dallas, Texas 75222-4076
Phone: (800) 207-0992
www.celebratinglife.org

The Celebrating Life Foundation (CLF) is a non-profit organization devoted to educating the African American community and women of color about the risk of breast cancer. It also encourages advancements in the early detection and treatment, and the improvement of survival rates among these women.

Hereditary Cancer Center (HCC)

Creighton University
2500 California Plaza
Omaha, NE 68178
Phone: (402) 280-2634
Fax: (402) 280-1734
http://medschool.creighton.edu/medicine/centers/hcc/index.php

The Hereditary Cancer Center (HCC) at Creighton University was established in 1984 in Omaha, Nebraska. The primary objective of the HCC is to conduct comprehensive research projects dealing with all types of cancer; HCC is devoted to cancer prevention by identifying hereditary cancer syndromes. HCC conducts surveillance and management programs to oversee the natural history of these hereditary disorders.

National Cancer Institute

National Institutes of Health
Bethesda, MD 20892-2580
Phone: (301) 496-4000
(800) 4-CANCER or (800) 422-6237 Fax: (800) 624-2511 or (301) 402-5874
www.cancernet.nci.nih.gov

The NCI Web site offers recent cancer information from the National Cancer Institute, a component of the National Institutes of Health. Comprised of 25 separate institutes and centers, the NIH is one of eight health agencies in the U.S. Department of Health and Human Services.

National Coalition for Cancer Survivorship

1010 Wayne Avenue, Suite 770
Silver Spring, MD 20910-5600
Phone: (301) 650-9127 or (888) 650-9127
Fax: (301) 565-9670
www.canceradvocacy.org

Founded in 1986 by and for people with cancer and those who care for them, the National Coalition for Cancer Survivorship (NCCS) is a patient-led advocacy organization working on behalf of people with all types of cancer and their families. Their mission is to ensure quality cancer care for all Americans by leading and strengthening the survivorship movement, empowering cancer survivors, and advocating for policy issues that affect cancer survivors' quality of life.

OncoLink

The University of Pennsylvania Medical Center
3400 Spruce Street – 2 Donner
Philadelphia, PA 19104
www.oncolink.upenn.edu/disease/breast

Maintained by the University of Pennsylvania, OncoLink's mission is to help cancer patients, families, health care professionals, and the general public receive accurate cancer-related information at no charge. OncoLink offers comprehensive information about specific types of cancer, updates on cancer treatments, and news about research advances. The information is updated every day and is provided information at various levels, from introductory to in-depth.

Susan G. Komen Breast Cancer Foundation
5005 LBJ Freeway, Suite 250
Dallas, TX 75244
Phone: (972) 855-1600
Fax: (972) 855-1605
Help Line: (800) IM AWARE
www.komen.org

The Susan G. Komen Breast Cancer Foundation is a nonprofit organization with a network of volunteers working through local affiliates and Race for the Cure events in cities across the United States. Their mission is to eradicate breast cancer as a life-threatening disease by advancing research, education, screening, and treatment.

U.S. Food and Drug Administration
5600 Fishers Lane
Rockville, MD 20857
(888) INFO-FDA (888) 463-6332www.fda.gov

U.S. National Library of Medicine
8600 Rockville Pike
Bethesda, MD 20894
www.nlm.nih.gov
MEDLINEplus www.nlm.nih.gov/medlineplus

MedlinePlus brings together authoritative information from National Library of Medicine (NLM), the National Institutes of Health (NIH), and other government agencies and health-related organizations. MedlinePlus gives easy access to medical journal articles and also has extensive information about drugs, an illustrated medical encyclopedia, interactive patient tutorials, and latest health news.

Glossary

A

ABBI (advanced breast biopsy instrumentation): use of a rotating, circular knife to remove a large sample of tissue for biopsy.

accelerated partial breast radiation: radiation therapy delivered to only part of the breast over a period of days.

adjuvant therapy: anticancer drugs used in chemotherapy, hormone blocking therapy, and targeted therapy, after surgery and/or radiation, to prevent recurrence or metastasis.

alkylators: a class of chemotherapy drugs that inhibit cell division and growth.

anastrozole (*Arimidex*): a drug used in hormone blocking therapy.

anatomical implant: a breast implant that is fuller at the bottom than at the top; also called a teardrop, contoured, or shaped implant.

aneuploid: having abnormal amounts of DNA; tumors with aneuploid cells tend to be aggressive.

antimicrotubules: chemotherapy drugs that directly kill cancer cells with minimal damage to normal cells.

antineoplastics: chemotherapy drugs.

antitumor antibiotics: chemotherapy drugs.

areola: the darker-colored skin surrounding the nipple.

aromatase: an enzyme that converts other hormones to estrogen; it is the principal source of estrogen after menopause.

aromatase inhibitors: drugs that block estrogen production by inhibiting the hormone aromatase.

aspiration: a procedure in which a hollow needle withdraws fluid from a breast mass or other part of the body.

asymmetrical: having opposite sides or parts that do not precisely match, as when one breast is larger or smaller than the other.

axilla: armpit.

axillary dissection: surgical removal of lymph nodes in the armpit area.

B

baseline: a condition against which later changes are compared, as in a *baseline* mammogram, usually taken before age forty.

benign: not cancerous.

bilateral: having two sides; affecting two sides equally, as in a *bilateral* mastectomy.

biopsy: a diagnostic procedure that removes tissue for microscopic analysis.

bisphosphonates: a class of drugs that disrupt the normal cycle in which bone breaks down and regenerates.

bone marrow: soft cell tissue in the bone center, where red blood cells, white blood cells, and platelets are manufactured.

bone marrow aspiration: the withdrawal of bone marrow to be analyzed for the presence of free-floating cancer cells.

bone scan: a diagnostic test that detects areas of increased blood circulation in the bone.

boost treatments: tightly focused, additional doses of radiation, usually given for a week or two after standard radiation treatments have ended.

brachytherapy: radiation treatment delivered to a precise location by a device implanted inside the body.

BRCA1, BRCA2: genes, which when mutated, are associated with hereditary breast cancer.

breast implant: a soft pouch, filled with saline or silicone, that is surgically implanted beneath the skin and muscle of the chest wall to form a reconstructed breast after mastectomy.

breast reconstruction: any surgical method used to create a new breast after mastectomy. The new breast will not produce milk and will not have sensation but will look like a normal breast.

breast self-examination (BSE): a monthly routine in which a woman follows several steps to detect any changes or suspicious lumps in her breasts.

bulb: the smallest component in the milk-producing system of lobes in the breast.

C

cancer: a general term for diseases characterized by uncontrolled growth of abnormal cells that can invade and destroy healthy tissue. Also called malignancy.

capsular contracture: a complication following implant reconstruction in which scar tissue around the implant begins to contract and squeeze the implant.

carcinogenic: cancer-causing.

carcinoma: the most common type of cancer, affecting skin, glands, or the lining of organs.

catheter: a tube-shaped medical device inserted into the body to keep a passage open or to facilitate the injection or withdrawal of fluids.

cell: the smallest structural unit of living tissue that can survive and reproduce on its own.

cell cycle: all cell activity from one cell division to the next.

chemotherapy: the administration of anticancer drugs that directly kill cancer cells or disrupt their ability to grow and reproduce.

clinical trial: a research project that tests drugs or other treatments on human subjects.

core biopsy: a diagnostic test in which a hollow needle removes small samples of tissue for laboratory analysis.

CT (computerized tomography) scan: a computer-aided method of creating three-dimensional images of organs and structures inside the body.

cyclophosphamide: an alkylator.

cytologist: a specialist who analyzes cells and diagnoses disease from cell abnormalities.

cytotoxic: toxic to cells; capable of destroying cells.

cyst: a benign, fluid-filled lump.

D

DCIS (ductal carcinoma in situ): a precancerous condition in which abnormal cells have been found in the milk ducts of the breast but have not broken through the duct walls.

density: compact, thick.

DES (diethylstilbestrol): a synthetic estrogen that was once prescribed to prevent complications in pregnancy; it is no longer used, because it increases the risk of breast cancer.

diagnosis: the process of identifying a disease from its symptoms and from tests such as X-rays or biopsies; in breast cancer, determining the nature of a lump or any other change in the breast.

diagnostic mammogram: not a routine mammogram, but one ordered to investigate a lump found during BSE or a clinical examination.

DIEA flap (deep inferior epigastric artery): a section of skin and fat moved up from the lower abdomen to the chest area and used for breast reconstruction after mastectomy.

diffuse: not localized in a single area.

digital mammography: a process in which the images produced on a mammogram machine are converted to computer code and then displayed in much finer detail than film can capture.

diploid: containing normal amounts of DNA; diploid tumors are usually not aggressive.

distant recurrence: a reappearance of cancer at a site other than the site of the original tumor.

DNA (deoxyribonucleic acid): the material that carries the genetic code, and establishes hereditary patterns, including inherited risks for certain diseases.

DNA repair enzyme inhibitors: chemotherapy drugs.

duct: a narrow tube that carries milk from the lobes of the breast to the nipple.

ductal carcinoma: cancer that arises in the milk ducts.

ductal lavage: a diagnostic test in which a saline solution is introduced into the breast ducts and then withdrawn so that cells from the ducts can be analyzed for abnormalities.

E

early detection: discovery of a cancer while it is still small—no more than two centimeters in diameter—and before it has spread to lymph nodes near the breast.

enzyme: a complex protein that supports or initiates certain chemical reactions in the body.

epoetin alfa: a drug that stimulates the production of white blood cells.

erythropoietin: a drug that stimulates the production of red blood cells.

estrogen: a female sex hormone produced by the ovaries, adrenal glands, placenta, and fatty tissues.

estrogen receptor: a location on a tumor at which estrogen molecules can attach; the presence of estrogen receptors means a tumor depends on estrogen to grow.

excisional biopsy: a surgical biopsy used for small tumors and capable of removing them completely.

exemestane (Aromasin): a drug used in hormone blocking therapy; it blocks estrogen production in postmenopausal women by inhibiting the enzyme aromatase.

expander: a soft, empty pouch placed behind the chest muscle and gradually filled with saline over a period of months to stretch the skin before a breast implant is put in place.

external boost treatment: external beam radiation therapy delivered to a smaller area after a course of standard radiation therapy.

external radiation: radiation delivered from outside the body.

external-beam brachytherapy: a treatment that delivers radiation to a tumor area but requires no catheters or balloons.

extrusion: the act of being forced through an opening, such as when an implant extrudes due to skin erosion.

F

false-positive: a test that erroneously shows a positive result.

fibrocystic changes: a common condition in which the breasts develop benign, normal cysts that are sometimes mistaken for suspicious lumps. Often called fibrocystic disease, this condition is not actually an illness.

filgrastin: a drug that stimulates the production of red blood cells.

fine-needle aspiration (FNA): a kind of biopsy in which fluid is withdrawn (aspirated) using a fine, hollow needle. In the case of breast cancer, the fluid is aspirated from a tumor, and the cells within the fluid are examined for evidence of cancer.

G

genetic: having to do with the genes and hereditary characteristics.

gluteal flap: a wedge of skin, muscle, and fat taken from the buttocks to be used in breast reconstruction.

goserelin: a drug that suppresses estrogen production in premenopausal women.

graft: to surgically implant living tissue.

guided imagery: any of a number of techniques used to visualize images or imagine sensations in an effort to trigger a desired physical effect.

H

hematoma: a mass of blood that collects in tissue or organs; breasts may be susceptible to hematomas after surgery.

Herceptin: a drug developed for women with HER2-positive breast cancer.

hereditary: genetically passed on by a parent or parents to offspring; the risk for some cancers is hereditary.

HER2/neu: a gene that helps control how cells grow, divide, and repair themselves, important in the control of abnormal or defective cells that could become cancerous.

hormone: a substance secreted by glands and circulated in the bloodstream to other parts of the body, where it exerts specific effects on cell activity.

hormone blocking therapy: the use of drugs that block or disrupt the body's production of hormones in cases where a tumor depends on those hormones to grow.

hormone receptors: a location on a tumor at which either estrogen or progesterone molecules can attach; the presence of hormone receptors means a tumor depends on hormones to grow.

hyperplasia: uncontrolled, abnormally fast growth of cells.

hypofractionated radiation therapy: an accelerated course of radiation therapy, with higher doses given over the period of a few days.

I

image-guided biopsy: a technique in which computer images are used to guide a biopsy needle to a lump that cannot be felt but has shown up on a mammogram; also called a stereotactic biopsy.

immunohistochemical staining: a process in which living cells and tissues can be analyzed.

incisional biopsy: an open biopsy in which a small piece of a tumor is removed for laboratory analysis.

industry-based trials: a type of clinical trial sponsored by pharmaceutical companies in compliance with FDA requirements.

inflammatory breast cancer: a particularly aggressive form of breast cancer usually treated with chemotherapy before surgery.

infusion: slow drip of medication directly into a vein.

inhibitors: an agent used to reduce or slow the activity of a substance.

in situ: a term meaning "in position" or "in its place"; a breast cancer that has not spread through the wall of the milk duct or lobe where it originated is called *in situ.*

internal boost treatment: radiation therapy delivered internally to a small area after a course or standard radiation therapy.

invasive: cancer that is capable of invading, or has invaded, breast tissue beyond the wall of the duct or lobe in which it has arisen.

K

Ki-67: a protein whose growth rate in cancer cells can be measured to help determine how fast a tumor is growing.

L

lactation: milk production in the breast.

lapatinib: a drug sold as Tykerb used as a targeted breast cancer therapy.

latissimus dorsi flap: a section of muscle, skin, and some fat taken from the latissimus dorsi muscle of the upper back and used to form a new breast after mastectomy.

LCIS (lobular carcinoma in situ): the presence of abnormal cells within a lobe or lobes of one or both breasts; the cells have not spread beyond the walls of any lobes. The presence of LCIS indicates a heightened risk for either invasive lobular or ductal cancer.

letrazole (Femara): a drug used in hormone blocking therapy; it blocks estrogen production in postmenopausal women by inhibiting the enzyme aromatase.

linear accelerator: the machine most commonly used to deliver radiation treatments.

lobe: one of fifteen to twenty rounded divisions in each breast; the part of the breast in which milk is produced.

lobule: one of several small components of a lobe.

lobular carcinoma: cancer that originates in the milk-producing lobules of the breast.

local cancer: cancer which is occurring only one part of the body.

local recurrence: reappearance of cancer at the site of the original tumor.

local treatment: treatment of cancer at the site of the tumor by surgery or radiation.

lumpectomy: breast cancer surgery that removes only the tumor and a surrounding margin of healthy tissue to be examined for cancer cells; also called a wide excision or partial mastectomy.

lymph, lymphatic fluid: a clear, yellowish fluid containing white blood cells that bathes body tissues and carries waste products away through lymph vessels.

lymphedema: a persistent swelling caused by excess fluid that may collect when the lymph nodes and vessels are removed. This condition can occur at any time after surgery, including years later.

lymph nodes: small masses of lymphatic tissue distributed along the lymph vessels and containing lymphocytes that filter waste products from lymphatic fluid.

lymph vessels: similar to blood vessels but with the purpose of circulating lymphatic fluid through the body and to the lymph nodes.

M

malignant: cancerous.

Mammaprint: molecular diagnostic test that is used to assess the risk that a breast tumor will spread to other parts of the body.

mammography: the use of X rays to examine the breasts for tumors or microcalcifications.

mammogram: an image of the breast created by mammography.

Mammotome: a biopsy that uses suction and a large tube to withdraw breast tissue; also called vacuum-assisted biopsy.

margin: healthy tissue surrounding a tumor, removed at the same time as the tumor for laboratory analysis.

marker: a mechanism that identifies, characterizes, or predicts.

mastectomy: surgical removal of the breast.

mastitis: infection of the breast.

medical oncologist: a physician who specializes in systemic cancer treatments.

menopause: the permanent cessation of menstrual periods, usually in a woman's late forties to early fifties.

metachronous: occurring in a series.

metastasis: the spread of cancer from its original site to another part of the body or lymphatic system.

metastasizing: spreading to other parts of the body.

microcalcifications: tiny, grain-sized deposits of calcium in breast tissue, detectable by mammogram; when they appear in clusters, they are a sign of DCIS.

microcatheter: an extremely small tube used in *ductal lavage.*

micrometastasis: the early spread of cancer from the original tumor by means of random, microscopic cancer cells that have not yet formed a mass and are generally not detectable. (However, bone marrow aspiration can detect micrometastases when the cancer has begun to spread to bone.)

microtubule: very small tubules within the cytoplasm of a cell.

microtubule inhibitors: a chemotherapy drug.

modified radical mastectomy: surgery that removes the entire breast and the axillary lymph nodes.

monoclonal antibody: an antibody derived from a single cell to act against a certain antigen.

MRI (magnetic resonance imaging): a diagnostic imaging test that uses a powerful magnet and radio waves to show differences in the number of blood vessels in various types of body tissue. Cancerous tissue tends to have more blood vessels than healthy tissue.

multifocal: having more than one location; a multifocal breast cancer is present simultaneously in more than one lobe or duct.

mutation: a change in a cell's DNA.

myocutaneous: comprising muscle, skin, and fat; a myocutaneous flap is taken from one part of the body to reconstruct another, such as a surgically removed breast.

N

negative biopsy: a biopsy in which no cancer cells are seen in the tissue or fluid removed.

neoadjuvant therapy: chemotherapy or hormone blocking therapy given before surgery to shrink a tumor to operable size.

neoplasia: the process in which a tumor forms.

nipple: the portion of the breast that protrudes and through which milk is drawn.

nipple-areola: the nipple and surrounding shaded area.

node-negative: showing no evidence of cancer in the lymph nodes. A breast tumor is deemed node-negative when axillary dissection or sentinel node biopsy finds no cancer cells.

nonopioid: nonnarcotic.

O

oncogene: a mutated gene associated with a heightened risk of cancer.

oncologist: a medical doctor who specializes in cancer treatment.

Oncotype DX: a diagnostic test that quantifies the likelihood of disease recurrence in women with early-stage breast cancer.

open biopsy: any surgical biopsy.

opioid: narcotic.

osteoporosis: a disease in which the bones become more porous and more susceptible to breakage as a person ages.

P

Pamidronate: one of a class of drugs called *bisphosphonates*, which have been shown in some studies to prevent the spread of breast cancer to bone or to treat the cancer effectively if it does spread.

pathologist: a medical specialist who analyzes biopsied tissue under a microscope and diagnoses disease from any abnormalities that are present.

pathology report: the pathologist's written record of the analysis of biopsied tissue.

peau d'orange: skin texture like that of an orange; a symptom of inflammatory breast cancer.

pectoralis minor: a small, strap-like muscle running from the outer edge of the collarbone to the top of the breast, sometimes removed during axillary dissection.

pegfilgrastin: a drug given in conjunction with chemotherapy to lessen its toxic effects.

PET (positron emission tomography scan): a diagnostic imaging test that reveals cell activity by detecting the different rates at which different cells consume sugar, or *glucose*. Cancer cells consume glucose more rapidly than normal cells.

p53 gene: a gene that normally acts as a tumor suppressor but when abnormal, may be associated with a high risk of breast cancer.

phantom breast: the sensation that a surgically removed breast is still present.

plant alkaloid: chemotherapy drugs.

plastic surgeon: a specialist in cosmetic and reconstructive surgery.

platelets: blood cells that aid clotting.

polygenic breast cancer: cancer that usually shows up in more than one member of an extended family.

port: a small, semi-permanent opening that is surgically implanted just under the skin. It is attached to a tube leading directly to a large vein. A port may be used when repeated injections are necessary, since it eliminates the need to tap a new vein each time.

preinvasive: malignant cells that are capable of becoming invasive but have yet to spread into surrounding tissues.

postmenopausal: after menopause.

premenopausal: before menopause.

primary cancer: a first-occurring tumor.

progesterone: a female sex hormone produced by the ovaries.

progesterone receptor: a location on a tumor at which progesterone molecules can attach.

progestin: synthetic progesterone.

prognosis: the likely outcome of a disease; in the case of breast cancer, the statistical chance of long-term, disease-free survival.

prophylactic: preventive; a prophylactic mastectomy is performed when no cancer is present but the risk of breast cancer is high.

prosthesis: an external breast form worn by some women after mastectomy.

protocol: a document listing all steps, procedures, safety measures, and research methods to be used in a clinical trial.

Q

quadrant: any of the four segments into which a body part can be divided vertically and horizontally.

quadrantectomy: a partial mastectomy involving removal of the quadrant of the breast in which the tumor is located.

quality-of-life trials: a type of clinical trial that focuses on issues such as pain management and chronic side effects.

R

radiation oncologist: a medical doctor who specializes in radiation therapy.

radiation therapy: a local treatment in which a radioactive beam is used to kill cancer cells in the area of the tumor.

radiation pneumonitis: a short-term inflammation of lung tissue caused by exposure to radiation therapy.

radical mastectomy: an invasive surgical procedure that removes the breast, the axillary lymph nodes, and the muscle of the chest wall; radical mastectomy is almost never used today.

radiologist: a medical doctor who specializes in the interpretation of X ray images for diagnosis.

raloxifene: one of the class of drugs called SERMs, used in hormone blocking therapy.

receptors: a cell or a group of cells to which the hormones estrogen and progesterone can attach themselves.

reconstructive surgery: the use of plastic surgery to model a new breast after mastectomy, using either breast implants or tissue from elsewhere in the body. The reconstructed breast looks like a normal breast but is not functional and does not have sensation.

recurrence: the reappearance of cancer after an initial course of treatment has ended; recurrence can be local or distant.

red blood cells: cells that carry oxygen, which gives the body fuel for energy.

retraction: a drawing-in or drawing-back; when the nipple or the skin of the breast retracts, it can be a sign of inflammatory breast cancer.

S

S-phase fraction: the percentage of cells that are dividing in the tumor at any given time.

saline: a sterile, salt-water solution.

screening mammogram: a routine mammogram usually performed annually to check for indications of breast cancer.

sentinel node: the first lymph node to which lymphatic fluid drains from the area of a tumor; therefore, the first in which spreading cancer cells are likely to show up.

sentinel node biopsy: a procedure that removes a sample of tissue from the sentinel node for examination under a microscope. If the sentinel node is free of cancer, the other nodes do not need to be removed and examined, and surgery is minimized.

sentinel-node mapping: locating the sentinel node.

SERM (Selective Estrogen Receptor Modulator): one of a category of drugs that block either hormone production in the body or the hormone receptors on tumors, thus depriving certain cancers of the hormones they need for growth.

side effect: an undesirable effect of surgery, chemotherapy, radiation, or other treatment; some side effects include pain, nausea, skin changes, hair loss, or fatigue.

silicone: a synthetic material used to encase and fill some breast implants.

simple mastectomy: the surgical removal of all breast tissue but no lymph nodes; also called total mastectomy.

simple bilateral mastectomy: the surgical removal of all breast tissue from both breasts with no removal of lymph nodes; also called total bilateral mastectomy.

spiculated: star-shaped; a spiculated mass on a mammogram should be biopsied for cancer cells.

spiral CT scan: a CT scan in which the X-ray beam rotates around you in a spiral; also called helical CT scan.

sporadic breast cancer: breast cancer in a patient with no known family history of the disease.

stage: the grading system for the severity of a disease.

stage migration: when breast cancer is identified as being at a different stage in its development due to new breast cancer staging guidelines.

stem cell transplant: a procedure for regenerating bone marrow destroyed by high doses of chemotherapy drugs. Bone marrow stem cells (cells capable of forming blood cells) are removed before chemotherapy and then reintroduced afterward to restore bone marrow and its production of blood cells.

stem cell rescue: drugs given to stimulate the production of bone-marrow stem cells.

stereotactic biopsy: a technique in which computer images are used to guide a biopsy needle to a lump that cannot be felt but has shown up on a mammogram; also called image-guided biopsy.

submuscular: the placement of a breast implant beneath the pectoral muscle.

surgical biopsy: using an incision for the removal of part or all of a lump or suspicious area to be examined by a pathologist; also called open biopsy.

symmetry shapers: products that can be placed in a bra to achieve a symmetrical appearance post-mastectomy; also called "balance shapers."

synchronous: occurring at the same time.

systemic treatment: a cancer treatment such as chemotherapy that travels throughout the body to destroy random, microscopic cancer cells that may have spread beyond the site of the original tumor.

T

tamoxifen: an estrogen-blocking drug used in treating and preventing breast cancer.

targeted therapy: administration of a drug created to target cancer cells.

taxane: one of several chemotherapy drugs that directly kill cancer cells with minimal damage to healthy cells.

temporary radiation implants: small catheters used to deliver radiation.

tissue expander: a temporary balloon-like device, made of elastic silicone rubber, used to stretch the skin in the breast area following mastectomy.

tissue expansion: a process in which a soft, empty pouch is placed behind the chest muscle and gradually filled with saline over a period of months; this stretches the skin to accommodate a breast implant.

topoisomerase inhibitor: a chemotherapy drug.

total mastectomy: the surgical removal of all breast tissue but no lymph nodes; also called simple mastectomy.

toxic: poisonous.

TRAM flap: a section of muscle, skin, and fat moved up from the lower abdomen to the chest area and used for breast reconstruction after mastectomy.

transducer: a microphone-like device that's passed over the skin during an ultrasound test.

trastuzumab: Herceptin.

tumor: an abnormal growth of cells or tissue. Tumors can be benign (noncancerous) or malignant (cancerous).

Tykerb: brand name for the drug lapatinib, used in targeted breast cancer therapy. It blocks the HER1 And HER2 genes.

tyrosine kinase inhibitor: a drug used in targeted therapy.

U

ultrasonography: the use of high-frequency sound waves to generate images of internal organs or tumors. Ultrasonography can determine whether a suspicious lump is filled with fluid or is solid; if it is solid, it could be cancerous and should be tested further.

V

vascular: of or relating to blood vessels.

visualization: the formation of visual images.

W

white blood cells: cells that fight infection.

wide excision: removal of a breast tumor and surrounding margin of normal tissue; also called a lumpectomy.

Index

About the Authors

Suzanne W. Braddock, M.D., has been a breast cancer survivor since 1992. She is a dermatologist in private practice in Omaha, Nebraska. Born and raised in New Jersey, Dr. Braddock received her medical training at the Medical College of Pennsylvania, Philadelphia, and at the University of Nebraska Medical School, Omaha. Dr. Braddock is the author of several scientific publications. She has a daughter, Gail. For more information about Dr. Braddock, visit **www.braddockfinnegandermatology.com**.

John J. Edney, M.D. F.A.C.S., a plastic surgeon in private practice in Omaha, Nebraska, specializes in post-mastectomy breast reconstruction and cosmetic surgery. Dr. Edney is the Chief of the Division of Plastic Surgery at the Nebraska Methodist Hospital. He is an assistant Clinical Professor of Surgery at the University of Nebraska Medical School, Omaha, and Creighton University School of Medicine. Dr. Edney and his wife, Pat, have three children—Christopher, Matthew, and Jennifer. Dr. Edney may be contacted through his Web site, **www.surgicalimages.com**.

Jane Kercher, M.D., F.A.C.S., is a general and oncological surgeon in Denver, Colorado. She received her medical training at the University of Utah Medical School, Salt Lake City, and at the University of Nebraska Medical School, Omaha. A native of Wyoming, Dr. Kercher now lives in Denver with her son, Matthew. For more information about Dr. Kercher, visit **www.SurgOne.com.**

Melanie Morrissey Clark has worked as a writer and editor for more than twenty years. She is editor-in-chief of *Today's Omaha Woman* magazine in Omaha, Nebraska and is also co-author of *The Fertility Handbook—A Guide to Getting Pregnant* (Addicus Books, 2002). Ms. Clark is vice president of Clark Creative Group in Omaha. She holds a bachelor of science degree in journalism from the University of Nebraska. She lives in Omaha with her husband, Fred Clark, and their triplets, Cooper, Sophie, and Simon.

The Stroke Recovery Book—
A Guide for Patients and Families $19.95
The Surgery Handbook—
A Guide to Understanding Your Operation $14.95
Understanding Lumpectomy—
A Treatment Guide for Breast Cancer $19.95
Understanding Parkinson's Disease, 2nd Edition $19.95
Understanding Peyronie's Disease $16.95
Understanding Your Living Will $12.95
Your Complete Guide to Breast Augmentation
& Body Contouring $21.95
Your Complete Guide to Breast Reduction & Breast Lifts . . . $21.95
Your Complete Guide to Facial Cosmetic Surgery $19.95
Your Complete Guide to Facelifts $21.95
Your Complete Guide to Nose Reshaping $21.95

To Order Books:

Visit us online at: www.addicusbooks.com

Call toll free: 800-352-2873

For discounts on bulk purchases, call our Special Sales Dept. at (402) 330-7493.